BARBARIAN
EUROPE

TIME
LIFE
BOOKS
®

GREAT AGES OF MAN

A History of the World's Cultures

BARBARIAN EUROPE

by

GERALD SIMONS

and

The Editors of TIME-LIFE BOOKS

TIME-LIFE BOOKS, NEW YORK

THE AUTHOR: Gerald Simons, a staff writer for TIME-LIFE BOOKS, has been an inveterate student of the Middle Ages since studying medieval history and the early Germanic languages at Brown University and the Graduate School of Arts and Sciences at Harvard University. His interest in the art and architecture of medieval times has taken him on extensive travels to European churches, monasteries and museums. He came to writing after long experience as a book editor.

THE CONSULTING EDITOR: Leonard Krieger, University Professor at the University of Chicago, was formerly Professor of History at Yale. Dr. Krieger is the author of *The German Idea of Freedom* and *The Politics of Discretion* and co-author of *History*, written in collaboration with John Higham and Felix Gilbert.

THE COVER: Replicas of medieval chessmen, the originals carved in walrus ivory, these stern rulers and warriors reflect the robustness of the Early Middle Ages.

TIME-LIFE BOOKS

EDITOR
Maitland A. Edey
EXECUTIVE EDITOR
Jerry Korn
TEXT DIRECTOR   ART DIRECTOR
Martin Mann   Sheldon Cotler
CHIEF OF RESEARCH
Beatrice T. Dobie
PICTURE EDITOR
Robert G. Mason
Assistant Text Directors:
Harold C. Field, Ogden Tanner
Assistant Art Director: Arnold C. Holeywell
Assistant Chief of Research: Martha Turner

PUBLISHER
Rhett Austell
General Manager: Joseph C. Hazen Jr.
Planning Director: John P. Sousa III
Circulation Director: Joan D. Manley
Marketing Director: Carter Smith
Business Manager: John D. McSweeney
Publishing Board: Nicholas Benton,
Louis Bronzo, James Wendell Forbes

GREAT AGES OF MAN

SERIES EDITOR: Russell Bourne
Editorial Staff for *Barbarian Europe*
Deputy Editor: Carlotta Kerwin
Text Editors: Robert Tschirky,
William Longgood
Picture Editor: Kaye Neil
Designer: William Rose
Assistant Designer: Raymond Ripper
Staff Writers: Jonathan Kastner,
Peter Yerkes
Chief Researcher: Peggy Bushong
Researchers: Nancy C. Newman,
Alice Baker, Kathleen Brandes, Alice Kantor,
Helen Lapham, Carol Phillippe,
Martha Selz, Sigrid von Huene,
Linda Wolfe, Arlene Zuckerman
Art Assistant: Anne Landry

EDITORIAL PRODUCTION
Color Director: Robert L. Young
Assistant: James J. Cox
Copy Staff: Marian Gordon Goldman,
Barbara Hults, Florence Keith
Picture Department: Dolores A. Littles,
Joan Lynch
Traffic: Douglas B. Graham

The following individuals and departments of Time Inc. gave valuable aid in the preparation of this book: the Chief of the LIFE Picture Library, Doris O'Neil; the Chief of the Time Inc. Bureau of Editorial Reference, Peter Draz; the Chief of the TIME-LIFE News Service, Richard M. Clurman; Correspondents Margot Hapgood and Barbara Moir (London), Ann Natanson (Rome), Maria Vincenza Aloisi and Joan Dupont (Paris), Elisabeth Kraemer (Bonn), Jean Bratton (Madrid), Tony Kelly (Dublin), Arne Bonde (Oslo), Mary Johnson (Stockholm), Knud Meister (Copenhagen), Traudl Lessing (Vienna), Friso Endt (Amsterdam), Robert Kroon and Alex des Fontaines (Geneva), and Franz Spelman (Munich).

Contents

Introduction

On the night of August 4, 1789, a few noblemen stood in the National Assembly at Versailles and renounced their feudal and seigneurial privileges. A revolution had begun, not only for France, but for all Europe as well; and soon other great political and social institutions rooted in the Early Middle Ages collapsed one by one, like a house of cards.

The famous "night of 4 August" signaled the end of a story that began well over a thousand years earlier. It began, Mr. Simons tells us in this book, on another night, in the winter of 406 when a ragged band of Germanic nomads—numbering less than the population of a small 20th Century American town—crossed the frozen Rhine into Roman Gaul.

These were not the first barbarians to cross the Rhine or to invade Europe, but their arrival coincided with the end of a long era that witnessed the erosion of the once-mighty Roman Empire; commerce withered, society decayed, Germanic tribesmen rose to positions of great power in Rome's army and government. The crossing of the Rhine in 406 was merely the final bursting of the dike, releasing new barbarian waves upon the crumbling Empire. It set off a chain reaction that led to the sack of Rome itself in 410. For civilized men of the time this was an almost inconceivable event, and to them the light of the world was snuffed out with Rome's fall.

For a long time, it was usual to think of the six centuries that followed as an age of gloomy and static barbarism. We know now that it was instead an age of great challenges and magnificent achievements, a time when the most essential elements of Western civilization—and, indeed, the very ethnic composition of Europe—hung in the balance. For the nomadic invaders and their descendants, as well as for the established peoples of the continent, a whole new range of social experience remained to be filled in. Europe was at the crossroads. By the mid-11th Century, the die was cast. Europe had passed from a conglomeration of wandering tribes to stable kingdoms; and it was on the verge of carrying its hard-won cultural and political dominion overseas, through the Crusades.

With accuracy and skill, Mr. Simons describes the full sweep of those six formative centuries. The slow conversion of the barbarian tribes to Christianity; the emergence of new political forms; the development of new standards of justice; the revival and expansion of commerce; the rebirth of urban society and education; innovations in art and architecture; these are part of his story.

The privileges renounced at Versailles in 1789—as well as the Venetian Republic and the Holy Roman Empire that were both brought to ruin by Napoleon—all had their origins in this tumultuous age. While they have perished, other legacies of the Early Middle Ages are still hallmarks of Western society, among them parliamentary or representative government, the system of courts and juries in countries influenced by English law, and the existing states of Europe. This book describes the struggles and hopes that gave them life.

KARL F. MORRISON
Associate Professor of Medieval History
The University of Chicago

Barbarian Europe

THE PATTERN OF LAND AND PEOPLE
DURING THE EARLY MIDDLE AGES

NORWE-
GIANS

ANGLO-
SAXONS

FRISIANS

BRITONS

NORMANS

FRANKS

BURGUNDIANS

LOMBARDS

OSTROGOTHS

VISIGOTHS

VANDALS

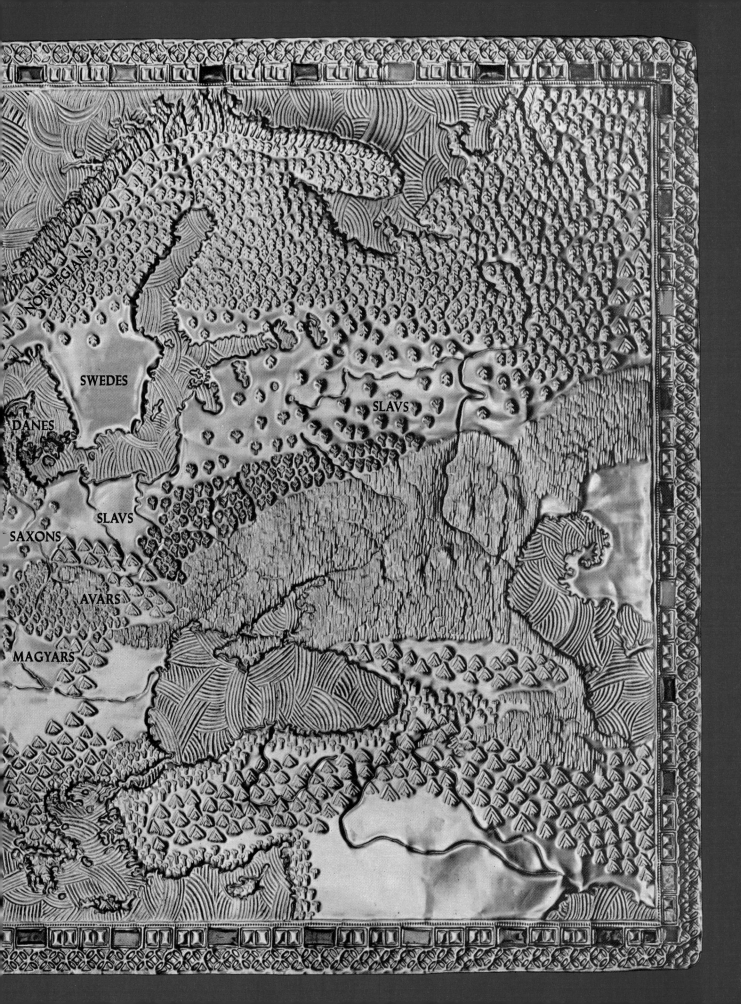

1

THE TWILIGHT OF ROME

In December of the year 406 A.D., in what is now West Germany, the weather turned bitter cold. It was a fateful cold, for it froze the watery barrier of the Rhine River into a convenient crossroad at the town of Mainz. There, on the last night of the year, about 15,000 barbarian warriors—along with their women and children and their farm animals—walked across the moonlit ice into the imperial Roman province of Gaul. Finding themselves virtually unopposed, the tribesmen spread out and headed south on a course of leisurely plunder and random destruction.

Despite its rustic and disorderly air, this invasion was a milestone in the history of the West. For the Romans, it marked the beginning of the end of their Empire. For these barbarians and many others, it signaled the closing phase of an incredible migration that had brought them, after a journey of centuries through thousands of miles of woodland and steppe, from their native land in Scandinavia to the regions that would be their new home. The ancient world was already dying and the medieval world was about to be born. A new epoch, now known as the Early Middle Ages, would soon take shape in the ruins of the Roman Empire.

Even today, the collapse of Classical civilization seems improbable—somehow too theatrical to ring true. How could an invasion of 15,000 vagabond warriors—and other incursions like it—make a dent in the fabled Roman Empire, a colossus of power and culture that incorporated the whole Mediterranean basin? How could those warriors hold at their not-too-tender mercies the entire population of Gaul—some 20 million people? For that matter, what conditions within the mighty state could conceivably make such an invasion possible? The unlikeliest reality of all—the sack of Rome itself in 410, only four years after the crossing of the Rhine—was viewed by later generations with even more amazement and dismay.

For centuries, Rome's sad fate distorted men's views of the barbarians and cast a pall over their whole era. Not until recent times, in fact, was the Early Middle Ages generally considered to be anything more than an unfortunate interruption in the rise of the Western world. This reaction, however short-sighted, was not altogether illogical. The

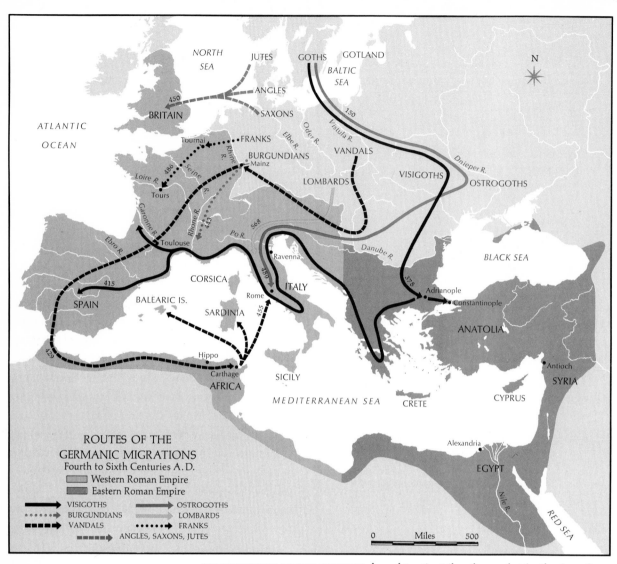

NORTH
SEA
JUTES
GOTHS GOTLAND
BALTIC
SEA
ANGLES
450
BRITAIN
SAXONS
150
ATLANTIC
OCEAN
Tournai
FRANKS
Elbe R.
Oder R.
Vistula R.
436
Seine R.
Rhine R.
BURGUNDIANS
Mainz
VANDALS
Dnieper R.
Loire R.
LOMBARDS
VISIGOTHS
OSTROGOTHS
Tours
Rhône R.
413
568
Po R.
Toulouse
Garonne R.
Ebro R.
415
CORSICA
489
Ravenna
Danube R.
BLACK SEA
SPAIN
BALEARIC IS.
Rome
ITALY
378
Adrianople
429
SARDINIA
455
Constantinople
Hippo
ANATOLIA
Carthage
SICILY
Antioch
AFRICA
SYRIA
MEDITERRANEAN SEA
CYPRUS
CRETE
Alexandria
EGYPT
Nile R.
RED SEA

ROUTES OF THE
GERMANIC MIGRATIONS
Fourth to Sixth Centuries A.D.
Western Roman Empire
Eastern Roman Empire
VISIGOTHS   OSTROGOTHS
BURGUNDIANS   LOMBARDS
VANDALS   FRANKS
ANGLES, SAXONS, JUTES

0   Miles   500

THE WANDERINGS OF THE BARBARIANS *brought entire tribes thousands of miles from Scandinavia to new homes in the Roman West. One of the most lengthy and circuitous of these treks was that of the Visigoths, who, in less than 50 years, traveled from the steppes of Russia, across the Balkans and Italy, to settle finally in southern France and in Spain.*

early medieval period was distinctly overshadowed by the ages that preceded and followed it. For sheer drama, it could not rival the collapse of the Western Roman Empire, a disintegration that was practically completed in the Fifth Century. Neither could it match the progress and pageantry of the high Middle Ages that began in the 11th Century and brought Europe new cities, magnificent churches and the spectacle of the Crusades. By comparison, the six centuries between the fall of Rome and the clear emergence of feudalism seemed singularly unproductive, an era in which man's best energies were devoted to mean pursuits, to futile violence and to subsistence farming.

The character of the barbarians themselves did little to allay this harsh judgment. Rome's Germanic conquerors made their debut on the stage of history as uncouth, unlettered, uncomplicated warriors—men who apparently loved battle and booty above all else. By common agreement among most historians, they stood convicted of two crimes against civilization: they had toppled the Western Roman state, and they had severed the golden cord of Classical culture. This condemnation was implicit in the name for their epoch—the "Dark Ages."

In the 19th Century, these views changed radically. Armed with new tools and employing new standards for historical research, scholars shed fresh light on the barbarians. Systematic studies of the records of great Roman estates revealed, for example, that their fortunes were already in steep decline long before the barbarians arrived. By the Fourth Century great areas that had once been cultivated intensely lay fallow, and farming was no longer a lucrative occupation. Yet by the Ninth Century agriculture was showing appreciable gains—under barbarian kings. Scattered farming communities were clearing vast tracts of land and repopulating whole districts long abandoned by their former Roman owners. Furthermore, they were exploiting a number of simple devices, such as the water mill and the heavy plow, to improve the efficiency of their labor.

The accumulation of more complete and detailed knowledge has now discredited the myth, and the very use of the term "Dark Ages." Rescued from neglect on the one hand and condescension on the other, the barbarians now stand forth in their true, bright colors. They were, to be sure, fierce men, much given to unpredictable rages, but they were by no means savages when they broke into the crumbling Roman Empire. For all of the lurid Roman tales of their atrocities, they were hardly more brutal than the Romans themselves; they displayed just as much capacity for kindness and generosity and, according to contemporary accounts, a good deal more fidelity to their wives. They were admittedly uneducated, and at first, as crude tribesmen, they were completely bewildered by the subtleties of Roman life. Yet as the accidental conquerors of an entire empire they were soon attempting willy-nilly to provide it with some sort of government.

For the next several centuries the barbarian experience was a classic example of a timeless process

—the meeting and merging of two peoples widely separated in levels of attainment. By this process the crude early Romans had benefited from their conquest of the sophisticated Greeks. By this same process today, half the world is seeking to absorb the technology of the West. It is a process to which the lesser culture often brings special strengths of its own—and so it was with the barbarians. As they were assimilated into the Empire, they injected energy, daring and ingenuity into a population practically bankrupt of all three. The barbarians contributed a genius for organization that galvanized the society of Europe. In the course of relinquishing their tribal identities, they stubbornly clung to their tribal attitudes toward law and the rights of the individual—and thereby preserved a priceless tradition until the time for democracy was ripe. Eventually they produced literary and artistic works now valued for their fresh qualities: a vivid and virile "primitive" Christian painting; a massive and powerful architecture, the Romanesque; and a robust and rhythmic poetry in the form of epics and sagas. Yet their age must be judged by other developments.

The Early Middle Ages was a political and social seeding time. In little more than six centuries the Germanic invaders created a new and vital society to replace a decadent one and transformed the Western world from a monolithic state facing the Mediterranean into a collection of independent principalities facing the North Sea and the Atlantic —the nucleus of Europe. From these raw, belligerent kingdoms rose the first modern nation-states and a civilization that led all others in personal freedom, economic development and scientific progress. The very concept of progress—the belief in the inevitable and continuous betterment of man—can be traced to ideas born in the barbarian epoch.

When the epoch began, the West had not only ceased progressing but was failing on a gigantic scale. The Roman Empire at the close of the Fourth Century was everywhere facing strains and dangers, and for years voices had been sounding the alarm, predicting disaster. As early as the middle of the preceding century, Cyprian, Bishop of Carthage, had written: "The world has grown old and lost its former vigor. . . . Winter no longer gives rain enough to swell the seed, nor summer sun enough to toast the harvest . . . the mountains are gutted and give less marble, the mines are exhausted and give less silver and gold . . . the fields lack farmers, the seas sailors, the encampments soldiers . . . there is no longer any justice in judgments, competence in trades, discipline in daily life. . . ."

Yet the Empire had grown great transcending crises and adversities, and its citizens, for all their forebodings, did not think of it as being on the verge of collapse. Like most people in any age, few Romans paused to consider the future in terms of the past. Those who chanced to do so might have been aware of the crucial nature of two decisions taken in their own time. In 330, the Emperor Constantine transferred his capital from Rome to Constantinople; and in 395, the Emperor Theodosius divided the Empire into two administrative districts, Eastern and Western. Though the acts seemed unrelated, both were inspired by the same purpose—to bolster the Empire—and both had the opposite result.

Time and geography were working against the Romans. Their monolithic state had for two centuries been losing its inner cohesion and its outward strength. By the start of the Fourth Century, its two great regions, so different in character, were beginning to pull apart. The smaller one, an arc of provinces that bracketed the eastern end of the Mediterranean from Greece to Egypt, was by far the richer and more populous. Its culture was predominantly Greek—cosmopolitan, urban, indus-

trial. The larger, the Latin-speaking West, was by comparison poor, rural, a commercial backwater. It served the Empire as a huge colonial territory, producing raw materials and products that were mainly consumed in the East. Even the rapidly growing Christian Church, which could have been the Empire's strongest unifying force, tended to split along East-West lines in its bitter arguments over doctrine and organization.

If the Empire had been able to defend both regions easily and well, they might have held together. But defense had become impossible; it was a problem as vast and complex as the Empire itself —and, like the Empire, measurable in miles. The Roman frontier was nearly 10,000 miles long. In Britain it was marked by Hadrian's Wall, spanning the island from coast to coast for nearly 75 miles. On the European continent, the frontier curled southward from the North Sea, following the course of the Rhine, then swung east to follow the Danube to the Black Sea. Encircling Asia Minor and cutting south through the Middle East, it embraced Egypt, and then continued across North Africa, to end at the Atlantic coast.

Outside this immense boundary, and exerting constant pressure against it, lay a hostile world. The Empire was threatened not only by the Germanic tribesmen of the Rhine-Danube region, but also by African Berbers (whose name may stem from an ancient Greek word for "barbarians"), tattooed Picts of northern Britain, nomadic Arab raiders and highly civilized, superbly organized Persians. Still another threat, and a terrifying one, loomed in the little-known steppeland stretching away from above the Danube to the Caspian Sea. There roamed the Huns, a host of fierce Asiatic warriors whose westward expansion late in the Fourth Century would drive a number of Germanic tribes hard against the Roman frontier. Though the Hunnish hordes were momentarily quiet, no one could guess when or where they might strike again, for "their country," as an old proverb said, was "the back of a horse." To guard the borders against all these marauders the Empire maintained, at staggering cost, an army ranging upwards of 500,000 men.

In 330, faced with mounting problems of defense, Emperor Constantine moved his capital from Rome to Constantinople. The decision was a brilliant one. It placed the seat of government at the strategic junction between Europe and the Middle East, on a military strongpoint that commanded the main crossroads of world trade. This tightened, through sheer physical proximity, the emperor's grip on his most valuable provinces, those of the East. Constantine's new capital, built up into an impregnable fortress, became the center of a glorious civilization that was to last a thousand years—Byzantium. From the rise of Islam in the Seventh Century until the fall of Constantinople in 1453, the Byzantine empire's stand against the armies of Islam saved the West from invasion many times.

But in one respect Constantine's transfer of the capital failed. It did not strengthen the whole Roman Empire; it merely strengthened the East. Constantinople's superb defenses, and its ability to buy safety by paying off would-be foes, soon diverted barbarian attackers to the West. By 395, the Western frontier was in such disarray that the Emperor, Theodosius, took the only course left open to him: he divided the Empire between his two sons. Arcadius ruled the Eastern provinces from Constantinople; Honorius governed the Western provinces from northern Italy. Each could respond quickly to military emergencies on his own frontier—or so Theodosius thought.

To the citizens of the Empire, this partition was nominal, a temporary measure to be ended when the current crisis was over. They had no reason to

A CLERIC VIEWS ROME'S FALL

Some newly Christianized Romans blamed the barbarian invasions on their own disloyalty to the old pagan deities. Church leaders—among them Salvian, a fiery Fifth Century monk—answered them by saying that the barbarians were God's punishment for the sins of Rome.

"Since almost all barbarian nations have drunk Roman blood and torn apart our bowels, why is it that our God delivered the wealthiest State and the richest people who bear the Roman name to the most potent jurisdiction of enemies who were once most cowardly? Why? Unless that we may acknowledge . . . that it was a question of merit, not of strength. . . .

"Events prove what God judges about us and about the Goths and Vandals. They increase daily; we decrease daily. They prosper; we are humbled. They flourish; we are drying up. Truly there is said about us that saying which the Divine Word spoke of Saul and David: 'because David was strong and always growing more robust; the house of Saul grew less daily'. . . .

"If human weakness allowed it, I would wish to shout beyond my strength, so that I would be echoed over the whole world: You, O Roman people, be ashamed; be ashamed of your lives. Almost no cities are free of evil dens, are altogether free of impurities, except these cities in which the barbarians have begun to live. . . . It is not the natural vigor of their bodies that enables them to conquer us, nor is it our natural weakness that has caused our conquest. Let nobody persuade himself otherwise. Let nobody think otherwise. The vices of our bad lives have alone conquered us."

think otherwise. Several times before, when the defense of the Empire required it, there had been similar divisions—and each time the Empire had been reunited. This time, however, the trend toward separation had gone too far to be reversed. Despite long and arduous efforts, East and West were never again wholly one. After 395 the West for practical purposes had to go it alone—fight its own battles, work out its own destiny.

The division of the Empire, like the earlier transfer of the capital, left the West weakened but with little cause for despair. Though it lacked the Eastern Empire's vast wealth, it did have a larger army. Moreover, it enjoyed greater internal unity than the Eastern Empire, for its people were less factional. Another asset was the Western Romans' long experience in dealing with the Germanic tribesmen. If Rome's superior military tactics could not contain the barbarians' assaults, then the guile of Rome's sophisticated diplomats would confuse their naïve kings.

Unfortunately for the Romans, this traditional view of the Germanic tribes was outdated. Roman-Germanic relations, once a simple matter of hostility, were now a complex tangle of fear and admiration, distrust and mutual dependence. Although the frontier remained as a military reality, it was now crossed often and easily in the course of many peaceable activities. With this increasing traffic across the line came an impromptu exchange of people and ideas. The result was a narrowing of the cultural gap that had existed between the two peoples since the Romans had made their first contact with the Germans.

When that contact had been made over four centuries earlier, Rome was young, strong and aggressive, master of an empire that already embraced more than three quarters of the Mediterranean world and was still expanding. In the middle of the First Century B.C. Julius Caesar, extending Ro-

man conquest into the Rhine valley, had clashed with some of the earliest Germanic tribes to migrate south from the Germanic homeland in Scandinavia. But the tribesmen he encountered were relatively few in number and so showed little promise of the might that was to grow during the next 350 years. According to Caesar's chronicle, *The Gallic Wars*, these tribesmen were a primitive, seminomadic people who lived off their flocks and did a little hunting and fishing to fill out their needs. By the end of the First Century A.D., however, the Roman historian Tacitus was describing the Germans as a more advanced people who lived in wattle-and-daub villages and practiced farming, although not with much enthusiasm. Their society was a simple one, explicitly organized for one activity, the waging of war. They had a king, chiefs and a tribal council of warriors who banged their spears on their shields to indicate approval. Their tribal leaders rose to power by winning victories and rewarding their followers with generous gifts of booty. For every man in this society, valor was the one indispensable virtue. Tacitus' description also included a classic inventory of the Germanic traits: "blue eyes and reddish hair; great bodies, especially powerful for attack, but not equally patient of hard work; little able to withstand heat and thirst, though by climate and soil they have been inured to cold and hunger."

During the Second and Third Centuries, the Romans and Germans were roughly in balance along the Rhine-Danube frontier. The Romans, their strength sapped by civil strife and economic decline, had long since abandoned their plans for extending the frontier and were now concerned mainly with defending it. The Germans, drawn south toward the Empire in ever-increasing numbers, had reached the frontier and were massed there. By the end of the Fourth Century, five major groups had emerged: the Franks, the Saxons,

The Lord's Prayer in the Gothic language shown below, transliterated and then translated into English, is taken from a Fourth Century Bible used to bring religion to the barbarian Goths. Bishop Ulfilas, who translated the Bible into Gothic, was himself a Goth. In order to write down the tongue of his people, he had to develop this alphabet combining Greek and Roman letters and Scandinavian runes.

ᚨᛏᛏᚨ	ᚢᚾᛋᚨᚱ	ᚦᚢ	ïᚾ	ᚺᛁᛘᛁᚾᚨᛗ	ᚡᛖᛁᚺᚾᚨᛁ	ᚾᚨᛗᛖ	ᚦᛖᛁᚾ
atta	*unsar*	*thu*	*in*	*himinam*	*weihnai*	*namo*	*thein*
Father	our	thou	in	heaven	be hallowed	name	thine

ᚢᛁᛘᚨᛁ	ᚦᛁᚢᚨᛁᚾᚨᛋᛋᚢᛋ	ᚦᛖᛁᚾᛋ	ᚡᚨᛁᚱᚦᚨᛁ	ᚡᛁᛚᚨᚨ	ᚦᛖᛁᚾᛋ
qimai	*thiudinassus*	*theins*	*wairthai*	*wilja*	*theins*
let come	kingdom	thine	let be	will	thine

ᛋᚡᛖ	ïᚾ	ᚺᛁᛘᛁᚾᚨ	ᚷᚨᚺ	ᚨᚾᚨ	ᚨᛁᚱᚦᚨᛁ
swe	*in*	*himina*	*jah*	*ana*	*airthai*
as	in	heaven	so	on	earth

ᚺᛚᚨᛁᚠ	ᚢᚾᛋᚨᚱᚨᚾᚨ	ᚦᚨᚾᚨ	ᛋᛁᚾᛏᛖᛁᚾᚨᚾ	ᚷᛁᚠ	ᚢᚾᛋ	ᚺᛁᛘᛘᚨ
hlaif	*unsarana*	*thana*	*sinteinan*	*gif*	*uns*	*himma*
bread	our	this	daily	give	us	this

ᚨᚨᚷᚨ	ᚷᚨᚺ	ᚨᚠᛚᛖᛏ	ᚢᚾᛋ	ᚦᚨᛏᛖᛁ	ᛋᚲᚢᛚᚨᚾᛋ	ᛋᛁᚵᚨᛁᛘᚨ
daga	*jah*	*aflet*	*uns*	*thatei*	*skulans*	*sijaima*
day	and	forgive	us	that	guilty	we are

ᛋᚡᚨᛋᚡᛖ	ᚷᚨᚺ	ᚡᛖᛁᛋ	ᚨᚠᛚᛖᛏᚨᛗ	ᚦᚨᛁᛗ	ᛋᚲᚢᛚᚨᛗ
swaswe	*jah*	*weis*	*afletam*	*thaim*	*skulam*
as	also	we	forgive	the	debtors

ᚢᚾᛋᚨᚱᚨᛁᛗ	ᚷᚨᚺ	ᚾᛁ	ᛒᚱᛁᚷᚷᚨᛁᛋ	ᚢᚾᛋ	ïᚾ	ᚠᚱᚨᛁᛋᛏᚢᛒᚾᚨᛁ
unsaraim	*jah*	*ni*	*briggais*	*uns*	*in*	*fraistubnjai*
our	also	not	bring	us	into	temptation

ᚨᚲ	ᛚᚨᚢᛋᛖᛁ	ᚢᚾᛋ	ᚨᚠ	ᚦᚨᛗᛗᚨ	ᚢᛒᛁᛚᛁᚾ	ᚢᚾᛏᛖ
ak	*lausei*	*uns*	*af*	*thamma*	*ubilin*	*unte*
but	free	us	from	this	evil	for

ᚦᛖᛁᚾᚨ	ïᛋᛏ	ᚦᛁᚢᚨᚨᚾᚷᚨᚱᛞᛁ	ᚷᚨᚺ	ᛗᚨᚺᛏᛋ	ᚷᚨᚺ
theina	*ist*	*thiudangardi*	*jah*	*mahts*	*jah*
thine	is	kingdom	and	power	and

ᚡᚢᛚᚦᚢᛋ	ïᚾ	ᚨᛁᚡᛁᚾᛋ		ᚨᛗᛖᚾ
wulthus	*in*	*aiwins*		*amen*
glory	in	eternity		Amen

the Vandals, the Ostrogoths and the Visigoths. From the outset, the Visigoths were especially troublesome to the Empire, raiding far and wide through the Balkans. At the same time, the Visigoths and other Germanic tribes along the frontier benefited from contact with Roman civilization.

One of the most important of these influences was Christianity. Around the middle of the Fourth Century, a venturesome bishop named Ulfilas—born a barbarian but raised in Constantinople—traveled among the Visigothic tribes north of the Danube, making many converts. He even gave the Visigoths a Bible in their own tongue. The so-called Gothic Bible was not complete: Ulfilas prudently omitted certain passages in the Old Testament that he felt would encourage the tribesmen in their warlike ways. His teaching, however, soon spread from the Visigoths to many Vandal and Ostrogothic tribes—and therein lay a major tragedy. Ulfilas preached a form of Christianity, called Arianism, which was unacceptable to Rome in that it minimized the divinity of Christ; thus in the eyes of the church, it made heretics of the most civilized of the Germans.

In their more mundane dealings with the Empire, the Germanic tribesmen were more fortunate. Enterprising Roman merchants had long been sending north gaudy jewelry suited to barbarian tastes, agricultural implements and household wares, wines to vary the tribal fare of curdled milk and home-brewed beer, and coins, which many Germanic warriors valued as ornaments rather than as currency. The Germans had one important commodity to offer in exchange, human beings—the captives they took in their internecine wars. Traders herded these prized chattels south and sold them into servitude as gladiators, domestic servants and field hands. Among them were thousands of Slavs—men, women and children—seized by the Germans in forays against the weaker tribes of northeastern Europe. In time, so many of these hapless people were toiling in captivity that their ethnic name, which meant "glorious" to them, passed into common usage as the inglorious "slave."

But the chief human export of the Germanic tribes was not slaves; it was their own free warriors. From the Third Century onward, Germanic soldiers enlisted in the Roman legions in droves. By the end of the Fourth Century the Roman army was predominantly barbarian, not only in numbers but in character as well. Soldiers from Rome itself adopted the hide breeches and cloaks of their barbarian comrades, went into battle bellowing the barbarian war cry, and sometimes fought in the barbarians' wedge-shaped formation instead of in the well-ordered Roman lines. Indeed, the very word *barbarus* became a synonym for soldier. The imperial military budget was known as the *fiscus barbaricus*, and a mother, writing of her son's enlistment in a Roman legion, observed nonchalantly that he had "gone off with the barbarians."

Not all Romans were pleased by this influx of Germanic auxiliaries. One vociferous group warned that "the shepherd cannot expect to tame the cubs of wolves." To other Romans, the cultural inferiority of the tribesmen was obvious and often obnoxious. Nothing reminded a Roman more forcibly of this than to pass some aromatic Visigoth, his long locks anointed with rancid butter—presumably to hold them in place. On the whole, however, the barbarians were not victimized by prejudice. Many held positions of high rank in the Roman army; some were welcomed as guests in aristocratic Roman households, and a few even married into them. Germanic men were admired for their size and courage and Germanic women for their fair-haired beauty. In fashionable Roman society, dark-haired ladies wore fancy blond wigs made of barbarian tresses imported from the north.

But despite the presence of so many Germans in the Roman Empire—and in the Roman army—the Empire was still unable to hold its frontiers against assaults by other Germans. In the hope of maintaining its borders, Rome turned to a risky expedient. It admitted certain selected tribes into the Empire as *foederati*, or allies. Under the terms of a treaty, each tribal group was given a grant of land and a yearly sum of money to be used as a stipend for its warriors. In return, the *foederati* swore loyalty to the emperor, agreeing to guard their stretch of border.

One beneficiary of this arrangement was a group of Franks who centuries later produced Charlemagne. In 358, after several Frankish tribes had suffered a severe defeat at "Roman" hands, they were legally

A CARICATURE OF A ROMAN, *complete with large Roman nose, was found scratched on a piece of marble in a Fourth Century villa near Toulouse. His dissipated, faintly greedy expression indicates how more than one Gaul probably felt about his Roman master.*

settled in what is now Belgium. Although they probably nurtured a bitter resentment against the Romans, these Franks continued to honor their military obligations—as long as imperial forces were garrisoned nearby.

The most powerful of the *foederati* were not the Franks but the Visigoths, a formidable people whom Rome treated so badly that it forfeited any chance of making the alliance a success. The Visigoths, after early forays across the Danube into imperial territory, had withdrawn to the north. But in 376 they suddenly reappeared at the Danube border, driven there by the pressure of Hunnish invasions in the north. Appealing to the emperor for sanctuary, they were duly admitted as allies—but never treated as such. Instead, the Romans treated the Visigoths as a defeated people. They were never assigned sufficient land, their weapons were confiscated, and many of them were enslaved. Callous Roman officials even sold them bad grain at exorbitant prices.

Angered beyond all endurance by this treatment, the Visigoths attacked a Roman army at Adrianople in 378 and practically destroyed it. They swept through the Balkans, helping themselves to what they needed—and often to a good deal more. In 395,

just as they had finally been mollified by the grant of lands in northern Greece, they were subjected to new tribulations: the division of the Empire into East and West placed the Visigoths midway between the two, alternately courted and attacked by each. This intolerable state of affairs was soon to have dire consequences for the city of Rome.

The Visigoths' troubles were acute, but far from unique. Throughout the second half of the Fourth Century, the Germanic tribes in general faced steadily mounting pressures—no matter where they lived or what their relations with the Empire. The arrival of each new migrant group from the north—impelled southward by enemies, failing resources in their homeland or simply by a desire to settle in a less rigorous climate—set off a chain reaction that displaced weaker tribes in all directions. Confederations were forged overnight by dynamic leaders, and just as quickly dissolved when the leader died. The tribes also lived in dread of the powerful Huns, whose westward drive had already engulfed some of their Germanic brethren—notably tens of thousands of Ostrogoths. To add to the unrest, there were droughts and epidemics.

But ultimately it was not war and disease that doomed the precarious status quo between the Romans and their Germanic neighbors. Rather, it was the desire of the Germans to share in the riches of the Empire. Despite the heavy death toll and the wholesale exodus of Germans into the Roman army, the tribal populations continued to increase and the barbarians could not produce enough to feed themselves—for this they needed more land. As warriors, their natural inclination was to get it by conquest. Sooner or later, they had to boil over across the Empire, reaching for the rich lands already under cultivation.

While the barbarians multiplied and grew more aggressive, the Roman West entered its final stages of decline. Decadence was visible in every aspect of

Roman life—in the sterile pomposity of its art and poetry, in the casual brutality of its public spectacles, in a rampant immorality that even Christianity could not check. The Western Roman economy, already undermined by the falling production of the great Roman estates and an unfavorable balance of trade that siphoned off gold to the East, had now run out of money. In some districts, money was so scarce that business had to be transacted by barter, and even taxes and salaries were frequently paid in kind.

The taxes, moreover, were crushing, sometimes taking far more than cash and cattle. The farmer might also pay a fearful price in personal liberty. Often unable to meet the assessment on his land, he escaped harsh punishment by deeding his acres to a great landowner and working for him as a tenant. Others fled their homes to live under barbarian kings or to join roving bands of brigands. Even the tax collectors (whom the Roman historian Salvian described as "more terrible than the enemy") were victims of the system. The law required them to deliver a fixed sum in revenues; if they were short, they were expected to make up the difference out of their own pockets. They could not quit their desperate jobs, for they were by law hereditary servants of the state. In despair, well-intentioned collectors became greedy functionaries in a bureaucracy so huge and corrupt that it inspired one Roman to comment, "Those who live at the expense of the public funds are more numerous than those who provide them."

Clearly the Roman West was failing in the very area to which it had made its noblest contribution: government. The Roman state and its administrative organs had ceased to serve their essential purpose, the maintenance of order and justice. Whether or not such a state was worth saving, the Roman people had lost the instinct to fight for it. While destitute and demoralized mobs milled about in the streets, and rich aristocrats celebrated wildly in their villas, hired barbarians fought to preserve their Empire for them—from other barbarians.

In the first years of the Fifth Century, a series of events turned Rome's decline into a precipitous fall. At the vortex of this crisis was a man who summed up in his person the central irony of the times. His name was Stilicho. By birth a Vandal and by profession a Roman general, he commanded the Western Roman army and for a decade had been the Western Empire's prime military asset. Skillfully conserving and deploying his dwindling forces, rushing troops to block assaults wherever they occurred, Stilicho had managed to stave off disaster. In gratitude, the Romans had erected a splendid statue to him in the Forum in Rome. A flowery inscription praised him for his bravery and fidelity, and noted the "exceptional love" in which he was held by the Roman people.

But Stilicho's best efforts could not postpone the inevitable. The Visigoths, turning their attention from the Balkans, were repeatedly attacking Italy itself. To defend the Roman heartland, Stilicho was forced to call home the imperial troops stationed on the Rhine frontier, leaving all of northern Gaul unprotected—except by the unpredictable Frankish allies. On the last night of 406, Germanic tribes led by the Vandals—Stilicho's own people—swarmed across the frozen Rhine. In their wake, the whole Roman frontier became a boundary honored only in the breach, and scenes of violence and destruction became commonplace in Roman Gaul. "See how swiftly death comes upon the world," wrote the Roman poet Orientius, "and how many peoples the violence of war has stricken. . . . Some lay as food for the dogs; others were killed by the flames that licked their homes. In the villages and country houses, in the fields and in the countryside, on every road—death, sorrow, slaughter, fires and lamentation. All Gaul smoked in one great funeral pyre."

SUBMITTING TO ROME, *a barbarian leader raises two fingers to acknowledge a pact with Marcus Aurelius.*

AN EMPEROR'S TRIUMPH THAT FAILED

It took nearly nine centuries for the crude, land-hungry Germanic tribes to infiltrate the Western Roman Empire, overwhelm it and begin reshaping its wreckage into a dynamic new society. At first the Germans staged sporadic raids on imperial frontiers. But soon some tribes became Roman allies and individual Germans joined the Roman army, ruthlessly fighting other barbarians who attacked the empire. A landmark in the long struggle was the war of 167-175 A.D., when a large-scale barbarian invasion was checked by Marcus Aurelius. To commemorate his victory, the Romans erected a 100-foot-high stone column engraved with scenes of battle, vengeance and barbarian submission *(above)*. Similar scenes of Roman success were to be repeated in following centuries, but in the end the victors became the vanquished and the Roman West became barbarian Europe.

Photographs by David Lees

21

Feared Enemies Who Became Welcome Allies

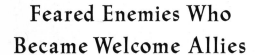

As early as the First Century B.C., during the rule of Julius Caesar, barbarian tribes had contested Roman power north of the Rhine River. Although these Germanic peoples were then no real threat to mighty Rome, troops often had to repel raids across the borders. To control the warlike Germans in the following centuries, the Romans used both force and diplomacy. Tribes living along the Rhine-Danube frontier were induced by offers of land, protection, money and gifts to act as buffers against other tribes, and individual tribesmen were enlisted in Rome's army.

These recruits were organized into auxiliary troops that served as scouts, reporting on the movements of hostile tribes and helping to contain them. The Romans respected the Germans' courage and daring in battle; they particularly admired the skill of the horsemen and recruited them to reinforce the Roman cavalry. Gradually these auxiliaries adopted sophisticated Roman tactics and learned the value of Roman discipline. When the first full-scale barbarian invasion came in 167 A.D., Marcus Aurelius' army included thousands of these Germanic soldiers, who played an important role in checking the invaders.

STORMING AN ENEMY STRONGHOLD, Roman troops link their curved shields overhead to form a "testudo" (tortoise shell) against a barrage of swords, stones and even wheels cast down from above.

Clearing the Empire of Barbarian Invaders

In the centuries before Marcus Aurelius became emperor, the Romans sent troops into the dark forests and marshes beyond the Rhine to fight the barbarians. Largely because of the unfamiliar terrain, these expeditions proved unsuccessful; as a result, the Romans concentrated on building border fortifications and establishing imperial provinces to separate themselves from the Germans who threatened the Danube and the Rhine River frontiers.

These borders were maintained until 167 A.D., when a loose coalition of tribes —including the Marcomanni, Quadi and Langobardi—suddenly stormed across the Danube and penetrated as deep into the empire as Northern Italy. For the first time Germanic peoples occupied Roman territory. Marcus Aurelius was so alarmed at this turn of events that he personally took command of the imperial forces— Roman and loyal German troops aided by allied barbarian contingents. The fortifications and encampments that the rebellious tribes had set up were stormed, and their flimsy log-and-thatch huts were burned to the ground. Overwhelmed by this onslaught, the invaders were slowly forced back toward the Danube border.

BURNING BARBARIAN HUTS, *a Roman soldier puts the torch to a tribal settlement, while one of his compatriots takes captive an enemy warrior who bears a decorated wooden shield.*

GASPING BEFORE DEATH (left), an unarmed barbarian awaits the final blow as two Roman soldiers carrying spears and shields close in on him. At his feet are his dead and dying comrades.

MORTALLY WOUNDED (right), a barbarian cavalryman slides from his mount, which had neither saddle nor bridle. Behind him a legionnaire stands with his arm raised to strike again.

OVERCOME IN BATTLE (below), a bare-chested invader, protected only by a light wooden shield, is no match for his Roman foe, who is outfitted with sword, heavy shield, helmet and breastplate.

The Triumph of Roman Might over Barbarian Courage

Marcus Aurelius' troops were able to crush the invading tribes because the struggle was pitifully unequal, matching the poor weaponry and raw courage of the barbarians against the superior might of the Empire's legions. Unlike the well-armored Roman soldiers, barbarian warriors wore neither breastplates nor helmets; they usually fought naked from the waist up, or with only a cloth mantle thrown over their shoulders. Their light wooden shields were easily splintered by the heavy, sharp steel swords and spears borne by the Romans; few barbarians could afford the luxury of swords, and their spears were made of wood, hardened and sharpened by fire.

Despite this ancient weapons gap, the barbarians' ardor was not dimmed. At the heart of their attacks was an enthusiasm for the fray. Charging swiftly into battle in a wedge-shaped formation and shouting wild war cries, they fought until overwhelmed, dreading surrender more than death.

Cruel Retribution for Those Who Challenged Rome

War against barbarian invaders was fought without mercy. Vanquished tribes expected no quarter, and got none. Their leaders were often banished or executed, and many women and children were sent into slavery. Some women so feared the conquerors that when their men were defeated they killed their children and committed suicide to avoid capture.

EXECUTING INVADERS *(left), Germans loyal to the Empire prepare to behead two captives. In the foreground lie decapitated bodies, while other prisoners, their wrists bound, await a similar fate.*

A TERRIFIED WOMAN *and her child (below) cling pitifully to one another as Roman soldiers lead them away to a captivity that may have meant a lifetime of slavery in Rome, possibly separation.*

Among the victims of this ruthlessness were the Marcomanni and the Quadi tribes, both powerful enemies of Rome. By the end of the year 175 A.D., Marcus Aurelius had defeated these two foes; thousands were killed, taken hostage or enslaved—often by other Germans who fought for the empire. Their strength broken, the Marcomanni and Quadi, along with other vanquished tribes, were settled just beyond the Danube River. However, they continued to harass the Romans, breaking treaty terms and helping other barbarians who fought the Empire. Eventually the Marcomanni and Quadi were absorbed by larger and stronger groups, such as the Goths, Vandals and Alemans, who continued to defy Rome.

A Victory That Failed to Save Rome

Marcus Aurelius had driven most of the Germanic invaders behind the Danube River barrier, and yet the barbarian threat was by no means ended. Regardless of how much blood they shed or how many defeats they suffered, the tribesmen continued to thrust relentlessly against the boundaries of the Roman Empire. In an effort to contain the barbarians and stabilize the border, Rome continued to make alliances with the Germans. At the same time the Roman government cleverly manipulated tribal politics, diverting the barbarians so they fought among themselves. Tribal leaders were even bribed with gold and favors; many of their sons were taken into the empire to be taught Roman ways, in the hope that they would go back and rule their peoples in the interests of Rome.

However, neither diplomatic stratagems nor military force could gain more than temporary respite from the Germans. Frequently Roman leaders mistook such lulls for permanent peace and stability. At the end of his successful campaign, Marcus Aurelius thought he had brought the barbarians under control. By his side stood loyal tribal allies, and the borders appeared secure. He could not have guessed that, less than three centuries later, the city of Rome itself would lie in ruins and all of Europe would be in barbarian hands.

A GRISLY TROPHY, *the severed head of a vanquished barbarian soldier is presented to Marcus Aurelius (seated) by a Roman legionnaire as a token of victory. At the emperor's side stands one of his Germanic allies, who looks on benignly.*

2

THE GERMANIC KINGDOMS

The period between 406 and 572, which saw the Germanic barbarians complete their migrations into the West, is undoubtedly one of history's most hectic and confusing epochs. As the Roman world crumbled, many tribes reached a peak of brief glory, or were obliterated in a nightmarish series of complex, little-known wars. To all of the Germanic peoples, this was their "heroic age"—a time of grand adventure and magnificent feats of arms. But in casual retrospect, the whole period seems to be one of patternless movement and pointless upheaval.

Beneath the turbulence, however, a clear and constructive process was at work. Everywhere in the West, new societies began to take shape as the small Germanic minorities mingled with the Roman or Romanized populations. From the first, these hybrid societies differed in ways that would have great consequences for centuries. They also had several common characteristics. All were ruled by Germanic kings. Nearly all were dominated by barbarian warriors who set themselves up as great landowners and substantial farmers; the vast social substrata of peasants and slaves remained virtually unchanged. Most of the realms were administered as before, by Roman functionaries manning the creaking machinery of the imperial bureaucratic system. The typical Germanic king thought of himself proudly—and not inaccurately—as an heir or successor to the once-mighty Empire.

Tradition is never quick to release its grip, and Germans and Romans alike were diehard disciples of the imperial tradition. Nevertheless, the period did produce a decisive change in the attitudes of both peoples toward the Empire, and toward themselves and each other as well. Throughout the West, the Roman citizens slowly relinquished the customs and ideals that identified them as Romans. The Germanic warriors were significantly modified by their increased exposure to Roman civilization, though they were scarcely beginning to pull themselves up by their cultural bootstraps.

Their greatest gains in this transitional period were made for them by their kings. These rough-hewn war leaders long remained captives of their outmoded assumptions of Roman authority. When they found themselves saddled with millions of

AN EMBLEM OF AUTHORITY, *this folding throne is thought to have belonged to a Frankish king. Such chairs, elaborately designed and cast in bronze or iron, served barbarian rulers and eminent churchmen alike in the Early Middle Ages, and could be transported from place to place like campstools.*

THE BARBARIAN TAKEOVER, *completed by the early Sixth Century, divided Western Europe among six major Germanic tribes. The kingdoms were loosely organized, however, and only the Franks survived the blows of continued invasions. From their domain come the modern nations of France, Germany, Belgium and the Netherlands.*

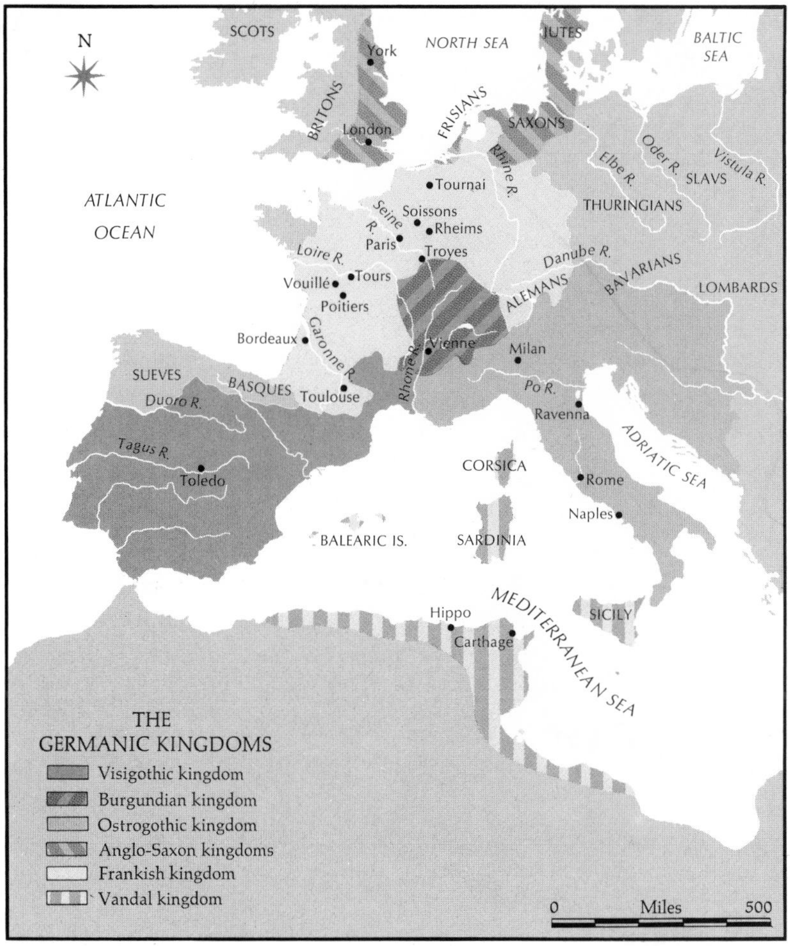

THE GERMANIC KINGDOMS

- Visigothic kingdom
- Burgundian kingdom
- Ostrogothic kingdom
- Anglo-Saxon kingdoms
- Frankish kingdom
- Vandal kingdom

0   Miles   500

Roman wards, most kings tried to rule them in accord with Roman law. But gradually, by a painful process of political pioneering, the kings learned to rule in their own names, without the benefits or restrictions of imperial tradition. It was through this process that the Germanic successor kingdoms (as they are known to historians) finally came into their own in Western Europe.

To a large degree, the salient features of each Germanic kingdom, and even its fate, were determined by the nature and extent of its founders' prior experience with Rome and the Romans. In general, the three major Germanic groups that reached the Mediterannean—the Visigoths, the Vandals and the Ostrogoths—developed quickly under the stimulus of their close contact with the Empire; but they paid a high price for their head start by bearing the brunt of the wars that ensued. The two main groups of Northern Europe—the Franks and the Saxons—were less exposed to Roman in-

fluences and to destructive warfare. They were slower to develop, but their kingdoms lasted longer. All five groups had left the common Germanic homeland in Scandinavia centuries before; and, traveling different routes, they eventually reached different destinations. In terms of modern regions the Visigoths occupied Spain; the Vandals, Africa; the Ostrogoths, Italy; the Saxons, England; the Franks, France.

As events later proved, the Frankish tribes had much the best of geographic good fortune. The Franks had been established in Belgium as Roman allies since the middle of the Fourth Century. They were close enough to Gaul to learn a little from its Roman civilization; moreover, their Belgian home served as a solid base when the tribes began their invasions early in the Fifth Century. Unlike the other major groups, which pulled up stakes and then started from scratch in some distant land, the Franks merely expanded into northern Gaul by means of a succession of small-scale advances. Because these modest early gains posed no serious threat to the Empire, the Franks managed to escape heavy retaliation from the imperial forces. The harried Roman authorities were inclined to forgive and forget the Franks' transgressions.

In this, the Franks did not reciprocate. They alone among the Germans harbored an important grudge against the Empire. The Franks probably owed their resentment to memories of oppression by one of the late Roman generals in Gaul; and their resentment may have intensified their abiding sense of independence and singularity. In composing a boastful preamble to their Sixth Century code of tribal law, the Franks proclaimed themselves "the glorious people, wise in council, noble in body, radiant in health, excelling in beauty, daring, quick, hardened . . . this is the people that shook the cruel yoke of the Romans from its neck."

In the first half of the Fifth Century, however, the pagan Franks hardly fit the description of "daring" and "quick"; "cautious" and "resolute" would have come closer to the mark. As late as 480, the Frankish kingdom was making only slow progress under undistinguished rulers. It gave no intimation of the fact that it would eventually become the most important of the Germanic realms.

The slow-going Franks were, nonetheless, considerably more civilized than the Saxon tribes, who had had but little contact with the laws and culture of Rome. When the Saxons started their invasions, their tribal culture was less Romanized than that of any other Germans. The territories that attracted the wild, pagan Saxons were in Britain—a province so remote from Rome that the Empire abandoned it early in the Fifth Century *(see map, page 155)*. The island was not only insulated by distance and the English Channel; its Latin culture was so superficial that, after the Romans departed, the native Britons reverted to their Celtic languages and their own tribal ways. The Saxon invaders—along with their close kinsmen the Angles and the Jutes—could develop their society with a minimum of both internal cultural resistance and external military interference.

Of the actual Anglo-Saxon conquest of Britain, few historical facts are known. But the meager literature on hand—scattered contemporary references, latter-day traditions and half-legendary accounts—permits a reasonable reconstruction. It appears that the early Saxon raids were followed by several invasions around 450, and that warfare continued intermittently for more than a century. The Britons put up a stubborn fight, but were gradually forced to give ground. Some fled to Gaul and settled on its Channel coast, giving their name to the Brittany peninsula.

The main body of Britons made a valiant last-ditch stand in southwestern England. Here they were given a final respite by the victory of their tough war leader, a certain Arthur, whose fame was embroidered six centuries later in the anachronistic tales of King Arthur and his Round Table of knights. But the Britons suffered a resounding defeat in the Battle of Deorham in 577 and as a result were pushed back to Wales and Cornwall. The westward thrust of the several Germanic bands now ended and a precarious order emerged from chaos.

The consequences of this piecemeal conquest—and of the conquerors' limited background—were precisely what might be expected. The various Germanic bands formed a number of petty, contentious kingdoms rather than a single realm. These kingdoms, whose names still cling to their general regions, included Wessex (West Saxon) and Kent, the domain of the Jutes; the whole miscellany came to be known as the land of the Angles—Angle-land, hence England. Haphazardly, the coarse kinglets and their boisterous warriors shaped the new realms in their own image. It was in England, more than anywhere else, that the Germanic invaders imposed upon the native population their own language, customary laws and farming methods. Only in England did the Latin tongue and the organized Church disappear almost completely. All this, plus sundry casual atrocities, earned the early Anglo-Saxons no love in England. One outraged Briton wrote them off bitterly as "a race hateful both to God and men."

Far removed from the Saxons, in terms of both geography and culture, were the Visigoths of the Balkans, a loose and wandering confederation numbering about 100,000 people. As longtime allies of the Empire, these tribes became the prime beneficiaries of Roman tutelage and the chief admirers of Roman civilization. But their proximity and great numbers also made them the clearest threat to Italy. Often unintentionally, and sometimes despite their best intentions to the contrary, the Visigoths were to haunt the Western Empire until its demise, doing more than any other Germanic group to sap Rome's dwindling resources.

The Visigoths entered their make-or-break decade in 408 under the leadership of King Alaric the Bold. Alaric was a bona fide hero of his people; but his boldness was not of the mind—and physical courage was no longer sufficient for a barbarian ruler. The king was a tradition-bound warrior, an old soldier in a confusing new time; and he lacked the imagination to use the Goths' great strength to best advantage, on the battlefield or off.

Twice before 408, Alaric had marched from the Balkans into northern Italy seeking food and land for his hungry, homeless people. Militarily, he was thwarted at every turn by Stilicho, the skillful Vandal-born general who commanded the Roman armies of the West. In Alaric's abortive attempts at diplomacy, he had been all too anxious to win

VANDAL-BORN STILICHO, *portrayed in an ivory plaque, rose to Consul of Rome and Master of Soldiers in its army. His dual role is suggested here by his weapons and patrician robes.*

Roman favor and a high office in the imperial army, and he was invariably out-talked or ignored. On one occasion, he sent a hopeless appeal to the Emperor Honorius, who was—as usual—holed up behind the marshes and barricades of his headquarters at Ravenna. According to Visigothic tradition, Alaric's envoys assured Honorius that "if he would permit the Goths to settle peaceably in Italy, they would so live with the Roman people that men might believe them both to be of one race." The Emperor was not tempted to test Alaric's sincerity; he declined the offer as brusquely as he dared.

But in 408, Honorius helped the Visigoths in spite of himself. Suspecting Stilicho of insidious plots and pro-barbarian sympathies, the emperor sent a band of soldiers to execute the general. Inexplicably, Stilicho made no effort to defend himself. Instead, he enjoined his followers not to interfere and impassively bared his neck to the sword. For good measure, Honorius permitted the mass murder of the families of barbarian troops who had settled in northern Italy.

To Alaric, the death of his wily old adversary was an open invitation to visit Italy again. With his warriors, the king marched to Rome and once again presented his demands for food and land. Finding the Romans uncooperative, Alaric starved them into submission in a bristling siege. Then he exacted an enormous tribute as his price for withdrawal: 5,000 pounds of gold, 30,000 pounds of silver, 4,000 silk tunics, 3,000 scarlet-dyed skins and 3,000 pounds of pepper.

Far more significant than this huge booty were the malcontents whom Alaric had picked up on his way. It was not surprising that thousands of the Empire's Germanic mercenaries flocked to the Visigothic ranks; they were deserting in outrage over Honorius' butchery of their families. But in addition, as a contemporary Roman wrote, "Almost all the slaves that were in Rome left the city day by

day and joined the barbarians to the number of 40,-000." This was no isolated phenomenon. In Spain and Gaul, too, oppressed slaves and peasants welcomed the Germanic invaders as liberators and unwittingly aided their takeover by rising up in revolt.

With his swollen host, Alaric besieged Rome twice more in the next two years. In 409 he was satisfied to blockade the granary at nearby Portus until the hungry Romans bought him off. But in 410, sympathizers inside Rome opened up the Salarian Gate, and Alaric turned the capital over to his warriors for three days of plunder—standard practice in the ancient world.

Alaric's historic sack of Rome was relatively orderly and restrained. But the intangible damage that it caused was immense and irreparable. To citizens in every part of the Empire, the inconceivable had come to pass: the Eternal City, which had been inviolate for eight centuries, lay prostrate before an uncivilized conqueror. No other event could have dramatized quite so forcefully the woeful weakness of the once-mighty Empire—and the terrible imminence of its demise.

For all of Alaric's colorful exploits, he had failed on his own terms: he had not provided his people with a legal domain of their own. When the old-fashioned warrior died a few months after the sack of Rome, the Visigoths elected as his successor the first of a new breed of barbarian king. This was Ataulf, a resourceful leader who took a larger view of the world and of his kingly role in it. Ataulf, too, was reverent toward the Empire; and like Alaric and Stilicho before him, he assumed that it was impossible for a German to take the throne and the awesome title of Roman Emperor. However, Ataulf planned to marry Honorius' sister Galla Placidia and hoped to sire an emperor by her; he was no doubt spurred on by the knowledge that Honorius had no imperial heir of his own.

Ataulf brazenly told Honorius that he wished

to ally his Goths to Rome and himself to Placidia. The emperor, of course, rejected the marriage, but his headstrong sister accepted. The wedding was celebrated in 414, Ataulf consenting to don Roman robes for the occasion. After the marriage, Visigothic warriors campaigned in Spain as Roman allies, in return for which they were granted in 418 a legal domain in southwestern Gaul, land which they had already begun to settle.

This operation had scarcely begun when the Visigoths suffered what seemed to be a national tragedy: Ataulf was murdered by a treacherous follower in 415, and he left no heir to the imperial throne. But the results turned out to be less than disastrous for all parties concerned. Honorius chose a new brother-in-law more to his liking—a general with a Roman pedigree—and gave him the hand of the grief-stricken Placidia, despite her disinclination to remarry. Placidia, recovering from her sorrows, enjoyed to the fullest her new life as the storm center of court intrigues at Ravenna; later, with equal gusto, she looked after the Empire for 25 years as regent for her son Valentinian III. As for the Visigoths, they prospered under the rulers elected as Ataulf's successors. They expanded through southern Gaul and began overflowing into Spain.

As the Goths settled down in Gaul, their presence caused many dislocations, but fewer real hardships than the Gallo-Romans feared. One of the biggest problems was the initial redistribution of land. The Goths made huge territorial claims, and justified them by invoking an old Roman tradition that allowed the military protectors of a region one third to two thirds of the land, or the produce from those "thirds." The Visigoths naturally chose their thirds from the richest lands, so their principal victims were the small minority of great landowners. To these aristocrats, civilization as they had known it came to an end. But the great majority of Gallo-Romans had little land to lose, and lost little.

Actually, the Goths' system of land settlement had conciliatory effects. In taking up residence on their thirds, the warriors distributed themselves widely throughout southern Gaul; they virtually abandoned their local tribal organization, relying on Roman bureaucrats to handle chores of administration that were too difficult for barbarians. Goths and Gallo-Romans everywhere rubbed elbows in the course of daily routine. Familiarity led to a natural accommodation, to mutual respect and admiration.

The practical Goths learned and followed the tried-and-true agricultural methods of the region. They quickly adopted the Latin tongue of the majority—so quickly, in fact, that in some areas the Goths' Germanic dialect disappeared within two generations. In turn many Gallo-Romans came to emulate the new barbarian aristocracy. Men doffed their togas in favor of breeches, and they lapsed into rough manners. Men and women alike made a vogue of the Visigoths' garish jewelry. The climax of this cultural give-and-take was more intermarriage, although that practice was legally forbidden.

The two peoples might well have been rapidly and completely amalgamated except for one thing: religious prejudice. The Goths' Arian Christian faith—ironically a Roman heritage—was an obnoxious heresy to most Gallo-Roman Catholics. Despite the general mood of tolerance, religious differences caused outbreaks of violence in Gaul. And in Spain, which was to become the Visigoths' final home, their Arianism met with much less tolerance from the more militant Catholics there. The results were frequent periods of mutual persecution that kept the two peoples divided for well over a century.

In the 420s, much of Spain was the stamping ground of the fierce Vandal tribes, which had arrived there in 409 after crossing the Rhine three years earlier. The Vandals, under pressure from the local Romans and the expanding Visigoths, decided to move on to the rich provinces of Roman North Africa; and in 428 they elected as their king the extraordinary man who would lead them there. He was Gaiseric, the crippled son of a slave. This proud, ruthless king was a gifted conspirator, a genius at political maneuver. For 50 years, Gaiseric's spider web of entangling treaties snarled the plans of Roman diplomats and Germanic kings—always to the Vandals' advantage.

In 429, Gaiseric ferried his whole people across the Strait of Gibraltar and led them east along the African coast. One by one, the gleaming Roman cities with their laden granaries fell to the hungry Vandals. The people of Hippo were rallied to the defense of their town by their bishop, Augustine, whose monumental work *The City of God* served as the theological cornerstone of the Early Middle Ages. St. Augustine died in his city during the 14-month-long Vandal siege; in the end, Hippo, too, passed into barbarian hands. The Vandal conquest of North Africa took a decade to complete. Mopping up operations were still going on when Gaiseric turned restlessly to a new project: he built a swift fleet and launched himself on a lucrative career of piracy in the Mediterranean Sea.

The Vandals' pattern of settlement in North Africa in some ways resembled that of the Visigoths in southern Gaul. The Vandals, too, carved out big estates and made their homes among the Romans. They, too, left administrative chores to Roman bureaucrats. But the relations of the Arian Vandals with the Catholic inhabitants were never better than strained. Gaiseric barely managed to hold animosities in check, and under his successors prejudice erupted into violence. The Vandals outpersecuted the Roman majority. They martyred scores of Catholics and provided medieval hagiographers with many a grim tale for their lives of the saints.

Gratuitous cruelty was but one symptom of the Vandals' swift degeneration after Gaiseric's reign.

The warriors, seduced by the luxuries that their rich land supplied, grew weak, corrupt and disorganized; and they succumbed quickly when their kingdom was invaded by an army from the Eastern Roman Empire in 533. Soon afterward, the Vandals disappeared as a distinct people, melting in with the highly mixed local population. They left little behind but lingering bitterness.

The Vandals' only real contribution was their unplanned but strategic role in the dismemberment of the West. Their initial disruptive thrust through Gaul and into Spain in 406-409 weakened Rome's grip on its outlying provinces, facilitating the advances of the Franks and the Saxons. Then, as conquerors of North Africa, the Vandals cut off the Empire's grain supply at will. This created critical food shortages, which in turn curtailed Roman counterattacks and thus helped all the Germans, especially the Visigoths, to secure their foothold in the Roman provinces. In addition, the dying Western Empire was kept off balance by Gaiseric's pesky pirate fleet and his double-dealing diplomacy.

In 434, however, Gaiseric and the other Germanic kings found themselves facing a formidable new adversary. Aetius, a Roman aristocrat, took firm hold of the reins of Empire on behalf of Valentinian III (the worthless son of the adaptable Placidia), and for over two decades his spectacular tactics slowed somewhat the erosion of imperial power. Like his Germanic predecessor Stilicho, Aetius was lavishly admired and constantly suspected—and with good cause. High-handed and utterly unscrupulous, he thought nothing of ceding a whole province to the Vandals in return for their support. Since Aetius personally retained vast holdings in Gaul, including some of the best lands not yet seized by barbarians, Romans found it easy to believe that he was protecting his own interests at the Empire's expense. Yet what was good for Aetius was usually good for the Empire as well; and though his motives could hardly be called patriotic, he was described with peculiar felicity by the famous accolade, "the last of the Romans."

In his battles against the Germans, Aetius added nothing new to the old Roman strategy of pitting one barbarian group against another. But he succeeded in escalating the conflict by tapping an unlimited reservoir of military manpower—the fierce Huns of Central Europe. Aetius had spent a period as a hostage among these Asiatic nomads; he and their leaders understood each other. Roman gold from Aetius brought down a Hunnish horde to crush a slave revolt in western Gaul. At Aetius' command, Huns inflicted a severe defeat on the Burgundians, a well-organized Germanic people who were expanding dangerously along the west bank of the Rhine River. And with particular relish, Aetius commissioned the Hunnish horsemen to belabor his favorite enemies, the Visigoths. To the Gallo-Romans, the Hunnish remedy might well have seemed worse than the Germanic disease, but Aetius continued to nurture his fine business relationship with Attila, the king of the Huns. Attila responded with utmost civility, even sending a gift to Aetius: his most exotic slave—a Moorish dwarf.

But in 451, Attila launched a Western campaign on his own behalf. His Huns burst into Gaul and swept all before them. Aetius and the Germanic kings had no choice but to make common cause.

The two great armies came together near Troyes (about 130 miles southeast of Paris), on a rolling expanse of plains. These fertile fields became—as the Visigothic historian Jordanes put it—"the threshing-floor of countless races." Fighting on the side of the Huns were several subjugated peoples, including the Ostrogoths. Under Aetius' command, the main force of Visigoths went into action with a motley host of Franks, Burgundians, Saxons (the cousins of the Britain-bound Saxons) and Gaulish Celts. Jordanes, writing with the true barbarian's

martial zeal, gave a rousing account of the day's gory work: "Hand to hand they clashed in battle, and the fight grew fierce, confused, monstrous, unrelenting—a fight whose like no ancient time has ever recorded. There such deeds were done that a brave man who missed this marvelous spectacle could not hope to see anything so wonderful all his life long."

The prodigious struggle (which, according to Jordanes' wild estimate, took 165,000 lives) ended in a virtual standoff—and thus as a victory for the West. Attila, apparently judging the cost of conquering the West to be greater than the prize was worth, executed an orderly retreat back across the Rhine. The great Hun revenged himself against the tottering Empire a year later in a devastating visit to northern Italy, but he died soon afterward. The Hunnish realm, deprived of Attila's strong hand, quickly collapsed. The West was left free to resume its domestic hostilities.

In 454, an entirely new phase in those hostilities was ushered in by dissension in the imperial ranks. Valentinian III, fearful of Aetius' ambitions, yielded to the goadings of the general's powerful enemies. Suddenly, during a discussion of financial affairs at the palace, the emperor stabbed Aetius, who was then finished off by a sinister eunuch. Thus a court gossip could say, with more wit than discretion, that Valentinian had "used [his] left hand to cut off [his] right." The friends of Aetius soon struck back, assassinating Valentinian.

This murderous tit-for-tat proved to be a Roman disaster many times over. The established line of Western emperors was terminated, as Valentinian was childless. And Rome, deprived of its leading general, lay exposed to the Vandals. Gaiseric the Lame landed his fleet near the capital, marched into the city and put it to the sack in 455. (This was but one of many times that Rome was sacked between 410 and 563; during the same period it was besieged no less than eight times and was held by conquerors at least six times.)

The Italian peninsula now fell into the hands of its own army of mixed barbarian mercenaries. Their generals, hoping to make their rule more palatable to the Romans, conscientiously installed and maintained a succession of nominal Western Roman emperors. This transparent imperial fiction persisted for about two decades, until Odoacer, a barbarian of uncertain origin, seized command. The new strongman boldly deposed the incumbent puppet emperor, Romulus Augustulus, a mere slip of a boy. Odoacer packed him off to a quiet villa and neglected to enthrone a successor.

This event, the so-called "fall" of the Western Roman Empire, occurred in 476; that year has since become the best-known terminal date in history. In its time, however, the event meant little. For all practical purposes, Germans already controlled the entire West. In a strictly legal sense, the Western Empire survived for four years more: until 480, a certain Julius Nepos, whom the Eastern Empire recognized as Western emperor, reigned in exile in what is now Yugoslavia. Yet even after the "fall," the Empire remained a very lively ghost in the West. No Germanic king challenged the authority of the Eastern emperor, and the Romans of the West were still Roman by law and Roman at heart.

Even for Odoacer, the Empire remained an inescapable reality. Although the general wielded the only real power in Italy, he could not use it effectively without the cooperation of the Romans. To win their support by legitimizing his rule, Odoacer sent a nominal pledge of subservience to Emperor Zeno in Constantinople and asked to be appointed Roman *patricius*—commander-in-chief. He received from the emperor a carefully hedged affirmation. Yet Odoacer clearly was an illegal king, and as such he had to be overthrown.

Zeno would not or could not spare the Empire's

Roman troops to oust Odoacer; but he was eager to see Germans do the job, especially if they had to fight to the last man. Zeno dangled Italy as bait before Theodoric, king of the Ostrogoths, a promising young man whom the emperor knew personally. Theodoric had been brought up as a hostage in Constantinople; here he had acquired some Greek and Latin learning and respect for all things Roman. Zeno found the king a willing collaborator.

Theodoric and his Ostrogoths invaded Italy in 489, and for nearly four years they had an unceasing fight on their hands. Odoacer's forces were whittled down only slowly—and not without subversion and treachery. Finally Odoacer made the capital mistake of admitting Theodoric to the besieged city of Ravenna under a truce. The two antagonists agreed to rule Italy jointly. Then Theodoric killed Odoacer with his own hand, and his men slaughtered most of the dead king's warriors.

With this less than noble act, Theodoric began a long and enlightened reign which, for its attempted restoration of the Roman life, might well be called the first Renaissance. The king propped up the dilapidated Roman administrative system, employing Romans as functionaries under their traditional titles. Like the Roman rulers of old, he engaged in public works, restoring seaports and repairing aqueducts, and he lent lively support to cultural activities of every sort. Theodoric made his capital at Ravenna and built there a flamboyant palace complete with glittering mosaics and grand columns transported all the way from Rome. Meanwhile he carefully maintained the legality of his reign with frequent shows of obeisance to the imperial authority in Constantinople. In one tactful letter, Theodoric informed the emperor, "Our royalty is an imitation of yours, a copy of the only Empire on earth."

But the modest splendors of Theodoric's realm were built on shaky foundations. In the main, the

Arian Ostrogoths and the Catholic Romans lived in separate communities, each distrusting the other. Disputes broke out that turned into national disorder after Theodoric's death in 526.

In Constantinople, the great new Emperor Justinian viewed Italy's disarray with more satisfaction than dismay. It gave him a fine excuse—though he legally needed none—for overthrowing the Ostrogoths; and it also promised him an easy victory. But Italy was only one objective in Justinian's ambitious master plan. The emperor mounted invasions to reconquer the entire Mediterranean West, and he appointed his brilliant general, Belisarius, to lead the initial seaborne strike.

Belisarius, with an army of 5,000 cavalrymen and 10,000 infantrymen, landed in North Africa in 533 and made short work of the decadent Vandal kingdom. Then he leapfrogged to Italy by way of Sicily and marched north up the peninsula (the same invasion route taken by Allied armies in World War II). Belisarius took Naples by siege and met little resistance in Rome. Throngs of Romans hailed him as their liberator.

Then, almost too late, the Ostrogoths pulled themselves together. They rallied around a fierce chieftain named Totila, who was proclaimed king in 541. Totila accepted the fact that this was a battle to the death against the Empire, and he burned his bridges behind him with two gestures of flagrant defiance. He minted coins which treasonably portrayed him in imperial garments; and he dispersed the Roman Senate, then a powerless body but one which nonetheless symbolized Roman power. Finally, Totila gave battle.

For more than two decades, the war raged back and forth inconclusively, piling devastation upon utter destruction. Finally the Ostrogoths were smashed in 563. At that point, the Roman Empire once more held Italy, North Africa and the southern part of Spain. But even then, the violence was not over, for the last of the Germanic invaders arrived from Eastern Europe to push the imperial forces out of northern Italy. These were the Lombards who, between 568 and 572, occupied lands as far south as the Po River valley. Simultaneously, the Visigoths counterattacked from northern Spain and began driving the Roman legions into the sea. Justinian's reconquest ended up as a bloody debacle.

Yet this destructive failure served a constructive purpose: it taught the West some lessons that it had to learn. The Arian Germans found out, at terrible cost, that they could not rule as agents of the Roman Empire; even their military power was not enough to assure them religious toleration. The Roman citizens, meanwhile, faced up to realities that were just as bitter. Their hopes for renewed imperial rule had turned to ashes. In Italy especially, administrators and troops sent from Constantinople had treated the local Romans not as liberated countrymen but as subjugated foreigners. This kind of Roman rule, far from fulfilling their hopes, was a good deal less tolerable than the enlightened despotism of Theodoric. In many ways the Romans of the West now had much more in common with the Germans than they did with the Greek-speaking Romans of the East. Few Romans of Italy were glad to see the Lombards come, but at the same time few could have been genuinely sorry to see the Easterners depart. Time and suffering had gone a long way toward reconciling the Western Romans to the Germans.

Though the Roman Empire was defeated and relegated to the East, it was by no means a dead force in the West. It would continue to awe the barbarians for centuries to come; its traditions and institutions would continue to influence them as they struggled along in an agrarian world practically denuded of urban life. But the dead hand of the past had finally been lifted from the West, and a new order was already in the making.

THE BARBARIAN SPIRIT

The waves of warlike tribes that swept over Europe from the Fourth Century onward dealt the death blows to a decaying Roman Empire and kept the continent in almost constant turmoil for more than half a millennium. But at the same time the invaders infused the West with a vigor of their own, which slowly melded with older traditions to forge a new Europe. Much of the spirit of these peoples—Vikings, Vandals, Goths, Saxons—is reflected in their rude but forceful artifacts, like the bronze medallion above, wrought with the figure of a mounted warrior riding down some unknown quarry, spear in hand. It bears the unmistakable stamp of the newcomers, who gave to Western civilization a new view of war and weapons, of nature and religion, and of the human spirit.

CELTIC HEAD, FIRST CENTURY B.C. TO THIRD CENTURY A.D.

Rugged Individualism and an Awe of the Unknown

For the barbarians, as for most primitive peoples, life was a constant battle for survival—against the stormy northern environment, against wild animals, against neighboring tribes. Such a life bred men of stubborn independence, like the anonymous Viking warrior whose fiercely mustached profile, carved in elkhorn, appears at center right.

It also bred men of fanciful imagination. In an effort to explain or influence the forces that shaped their lives, the barbarian peoples devised myths and legends, cults and gods. Frequently these gods were in their own fierce image, like the Celtic deity Cernunnos, whose powerful, magnificently whiskered visage is seen above. Other, later incarnations of the supernatural expressed the barbarians' feeling for mysticism: the massive-headed little figure at far right combines the forbidding features of a pagan idol with cryptic Early Christian markings on its chest.

VIKING HEAD, 11TH CENTURY

CELTIC FIGURE, NINTH CENTURY

45

An Admiration of Eagles

In their extraordinary wanderings, the various barbarian peoples left their footprints on four continents, crisscrossing all of Europe, traversing and settling North Africa, penetrating western Asia, even sailing the perilous North Atlantic to reach the New World five centuries before Columbus. It is

ANGLO-SAXON SHIELD ORNAMENTS, SEVENTH CENTURY

hardly surprising that such swift and mobile warriors liked to compare themselves to birds, and fashioned many of their symbols in admiration of the soaring creatures of the sky.

Above all the eagle, whose sudden, swooping attacks they so often emulated, held a special place in their imaginations, and was frequently represented in ornaments like those below. At the bottom are two shield ornaments that emphasize the fierce, curving beak and sharp, grasping talons of a bird of prey. The buckle above them, made of colored glass set in gold, depicts a more fanciful creature—a two-headed bird.

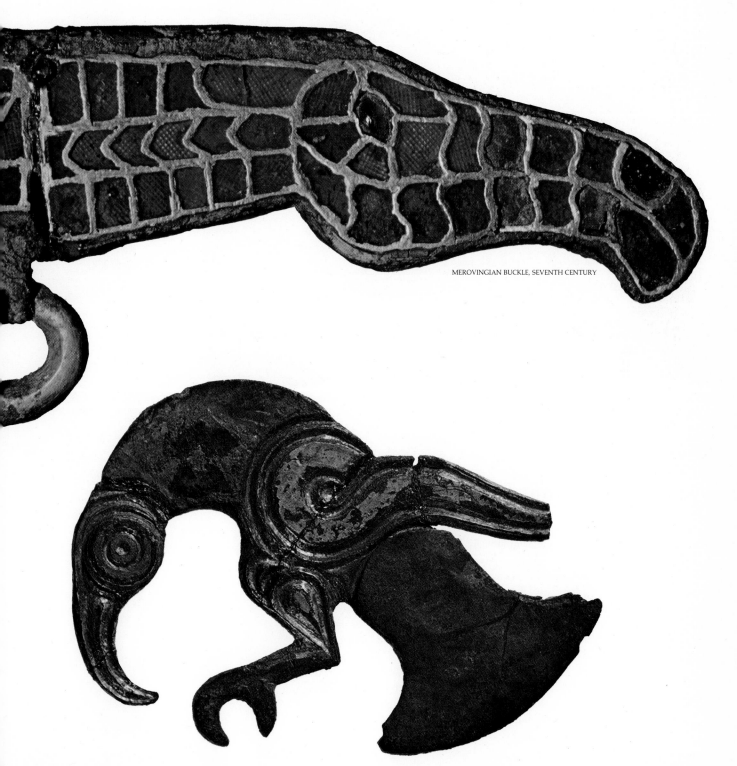

MEROVINGIAN BUCKLE, SEVENTH CENTURY

VIKING PLAQUE, SEVENTH CENTURY

A Superstitious Fear and Reverence of Beasts

Although the seminomadic barbarians raised herds of live-stock, and sometimes stayed in one place long enough to till the soil, wild animals were still essential as sources of food and clothing. Thus the creatures of the field and forest, which both sustained life and threatened it, quite naturally became part of the barbarians' religion. Animals, such as bears and wolves, were used to symbolize deities, and warriors often dressed as animals for ritual dances—as in the small bronze plaque above, which shows one spear-bearing warrior wearing a helmet decorated with horns, and the other a wolfskin. Another recurrent theme, that of man triumphing over beast, is illustrated in the plaque at the right, in which a hunter manages to hold his own against two fierce bears at once.

VIKING PLAQUE, SEVENTH CENTURY

ANGLO-SAXON BOX LID, SEVENTH CENTURY

A Passion For Warfare

The life of a barbarian, whether he was resisting inroads from other tribes or seeking new lands of his own, involved almost constant fighting. Virtually from the time a boy was born he was groomed to become a warrior. While Roman youths achieving manhood were given togas—symbols of citizenship in an orderly empire—barbarian boys, on coming of age,

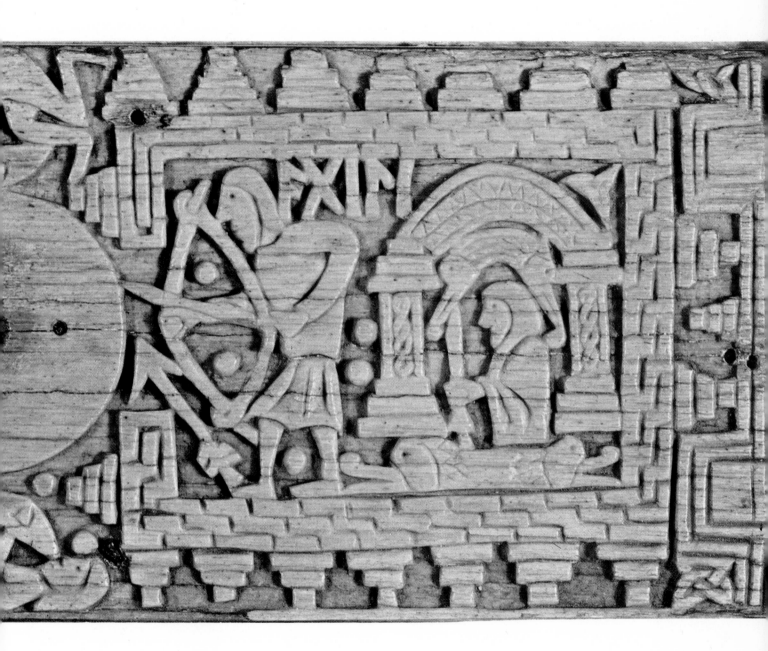

received their first weapons. This reliance on the force of arms left its mark on the face of Europe; it led to the fragmentation of the continent into hundreds of small, independent states, which were transformed into compact, self-sufficient strongholds that could be defended against conquest.

One such tribal skirmish is illustrated on the whalebone carving above, from the lid of a casket from Northumbria (the round object at center is part of the handle). Egill, a Norse folk hero known as the "master bowman of the North," defends his castle, showering arrows on attackers *(left)*, who advance with shields and spears. One warrior has fallen *(bottom, center)*, and over him a distraught woman weeps.

VIKING HELMET, SEVENTH CENTURY

A Pride in Arms and Armor

Above all other possessions, the barbarians treasured their tools of war, often endowing them with supernatural powers. Many legends tell of swords inhabited by demons, or acting as the agents of gods. The arms and armor shown here—a superbly wrought iron helmet trimmed with bronze, and two ornamented swords—were used by Vikings; the Saxons favored a two-edged dagger called a seax (from which came their name), and the Franks threw hand axes.

It was not only the adept use of weapons that made the northern tribes such formidable opponents. Their ferocity and their hit-and-run tactics often confounded the Romans, who were used to orderly ranks of men meeting in pitched battles. Sidonius, the Fifth Century Bishop of Auvergne, reported that the Frankish spearmen "closed so swiftly that they seemed to fly even faster than their darts."

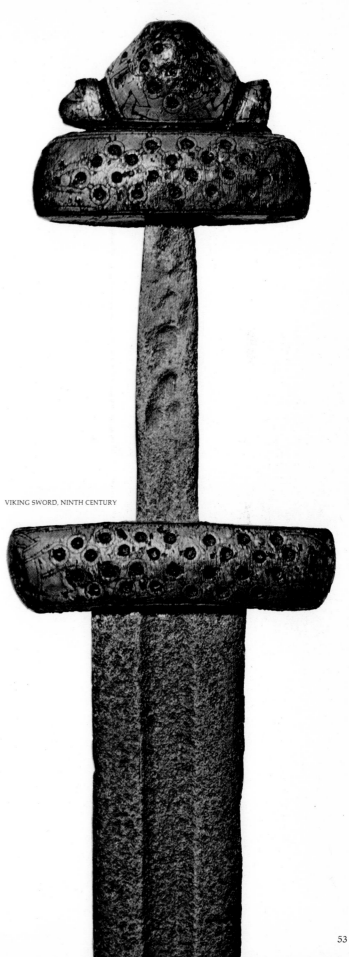

VIKING SWORD, NINTH CENTURY

VIKING SWORD, 10TH CENTURY

A Love of Splendor and Rich Design

As the barbarians settled among the peoples they had conquered, they adopted the customs, styles and religion of their former foes. This assimilation was reflected in their art, particularly jewelry, which became a fusion of Roman Classicism, Byzantine opulence and the barbarians' own crude vitality and love of color.

The pin at left combines the stylized bird motif popular among Germanic peoples with a Christian cross; the filigreed metal work, set with garnets, was undoubtedly borrowed from Byzantine artwork. Similarly, the opulent Visigothic crown at right reveals a barbarian admiration of massive precious stones as well as some refinements of Eastern design; the gold filigree, encrusted with sapphires and pearls, and the dangling pendants of rock crystal are of Byzantine origin. The hanging letters spell the name of King Recceswinth, a ruler in Spain during the Seventh Century. He is believed to have given the crown to the Church that converted him.

OSTROGOTHIC CLOAK PIN, FIFTH CENTURY

VISIGOTHIC CROWN, SEVENTH CENTURY

3

KINGS AND CLERICS

The foundations of medieval civilization were laid by a unique political revolution between the early Fifth Century and the late Eighth Century. Western society, no longer able to maintain its framework of Roman government, reorganized itself on the basis of Christian principle. The new entity was Christendom, a mystical commonwealth that united all believers across the shifting boundaries of the barbarian kingdoms. Faith was the patriotism of the new order.

This revolution was inspired and engineered by the Church. No other agency in the West, during or long after the Empire's collapse, could have filled the political vacuum left by the weak Roman emperors and unequipped Germanic kings. The Church alone had a constructive attitude toward society and an organization capable of putting theory into practice. Moved to serve the general welfare by an unshakable conviction in its mission to all mankind, the Church took the lead in the West, with political results as significant as its later contributions to art, architecture and the revival of learning. The Church provided and worked to instill social ideals and moral values. It brought the West under the great civilizing influence of Christian doctrine. It furnished trained personnel who sustained civil government while the barbarians made their painful transition from a seminomadic existence to a more-or-less settled agrarian life. These and other achievements proved so decisive that it is almost impossible to imagine what course Western history might have taken if the Church had fallen along with the Roman Empire.

The Church prepared for its role as leader by making significant gains in the last century of Roman rule. Benefiting from the establishment of Christianity as the state religion of the Empire, the Roman Church grew rapidly into a wealthy, well-staffed group of self-governing regional Churches. It also managed to rid itself of major heresies by the early Fifth Century so that everywhere it taught the same beliefs. (The Arian heresy did persist among many Germanic peoples, but as an external Christian rival to the Church rather than a disruptive force within the Church.) This uniformity of religious teaching was possible because the Western Churches generally accepted the pope's

A RAMPANT LION, *symbol of St. Mark, appears in a book of gospels used in spreading Christianity among Europe's barbarian tribes. The book was designed about 690 for St. Willibrord, an Anglo-Saxon monk who preached the Faith to the Frisians living near the mouth of the Rhine.*

views on questions involving doctrine. The popes claimed even broader authority, maintaining their right to set standards for Church conduct as well as doctrine. Both these powers, the popes declared, were their inheritance from St. Peter under the so-called Petrine doctrine, which was based on scripture (Christ's statement, "Thou art Peter, and upon this rock I will build my church") and on the tradition that St. Peter was the first bishop of Rome.

In the Fifth Century, the Petrine theory remained largely theoretical. By asserting their alleged primacy in the Eastern Empire, the popes steadily alienated the Greek Church, and even in the West they had no real political control over any regional Church, including those of Italy.

Within the Church, regional autonomy began as a logical and advantageous development. Christianity was originally an urban phenomenon, and the first churches sprang up in populous administrative centers of the Empire. Due to their location and seniority, these centers (among them Milan, Bordeaux and Lyons) became the episcopal seats for the expanding Church, and ecclesiastical organization was modeled after the Empire's provincial system. This arrangement placed the bishops in the middle of things, where each could respond swiftly to any emergencies in his district. As the Empire crumbled and its officials abandoned their posts in droves, the bishops were on hand to take over essential functions, and their experience at ecclesiastical administration equipped them to carry out their new secular chores with professional competence.

When the barbarian invaders arrived, the bishops were already firmly entrenched, confident in their multiple powers as God's vicars, spokesmen for the Roman people and trustees for the bankrupt Empire. To the superstitious warriors, the bishops seemed magicians and miracle-workers—awesome beings to be treated with respect or given a wide berth. But the Germanic kings and the

Roman bishops could not avoid each other, nor could they wish away their urgent need for what the other possessed in ample measure. Without enlisting the bishops' good will, statecraft and trained personnel, the crude kings could hardly rule the Romans at all, much less enjoy the benefits of their conquest. The bishops, on the other hand, could not protect their people and Church property without enlisting the kings' raw force to correct wrongs and to curb unruly warriors.

Mutual self-interest led kings and bishops into a wary alliance that would remain a dominant factor of political life throughout the Middle Ages. The kings, according the bishops great respect, sought their advice and often honored their requests. The bishops, broadening their secular activities, served the kings as mentors, judges, diplomats and top administrators—and thereby increased their influence in the Church's behalf. Many bishops even cooperated—albeit as a reluctant expedient—with kings of the heretical Arian faith.

It was the Arian problem that presented the Roman Church with its first crisis of postimperial times. By the eighth decade of the Fifth Century, Arian Germans had occupied all the Mediterranean provinces and they bid fair to sweep all of the continental West. The most severe Arian threat came from the Visigoths. Their realm, which was just then reaching its territorial limit, extended across southern Gaul as far east as the Rhone River and as far north as the Loire, and included most of Spain, as well. To stem the rising Arian tide, the Church had to pick out and develop a Germanic champion from a very skimpy field of pagan tribes. The only real candidate was the crude Franks of northeastern Gaul.

Consequently, the Catholic bishops of Gaul took an aggressive interest in the person and progress of a 15-year-old pagan warrior who became king of the Franks in 481. His name was Clovis (a variant of Louis and Ludwig), and he was one of the royal Merovingians, a line of chieftains initiated by his grandfather Merovech who, in Frankish legend, was said to have been descended from a sea serpent. Clovis proved to be the archetypal barbarian. Brutal, ignorant and totally amoral, he stole treasure, split skulls and collected concubines with alarming gusto. But this violent stripling soon satisfied the bishops of his outstanding qualities as a war leader. In the first half of his 30-year reign, Clovis hammered his scattered warriors into a strong army and, by piecemeal conquest, pushed his kingdom eastward to the Rhine and westward to the Atlantic. These victories brought him face to face with the Visigoths all along the Loire.

During these conquests the long-haired king was shrewdly cultivating his episcopal tutors, particularly the august Bishop Remi of Rheims. Perhaps Clovis foresaw from the start the advantages that would accrue to him if he became the only Catholic king in the West; at the very least, he recognized the divisive effects of Arianism on the realms to the south, and steered a safe course away from the heresy. In either case, Clovis in 493 scored a major diplomatic triumph in his extraordinary choice of a bride. Foregoing the more obvious benefits of a marriage to a royal daughter of the Visigoths or other Arians, Clovis wed the Burgundian princess Clothilde, a Catholic. With this rare queen encouraging her spouse, the courtship of Clovis and the bishops soon reached its logical culmination in the baptism of the king.

According to Bishop Gregory of Tours, who wrote late in the Sixth Century, the ceremony was performed in 496 by Remi of Rheims; amid a garish display of Christian pomp and pagan militarism, Clovis was followed to the font by no less than 3,000 warriors. The royal example started the steady conversion of the whole Frankish people and speeded their ethnic fusion with the Roman citizen-ry of Gaul. But the immediate results of Clovis' baptism were even more dramatic. The bishops of Gaul hailed Clovis as a son, and their slow-growing cooperation with the Franks blossomed overnight into enthusiastic support. What was more, pro-Frankish sentiment rose sharply among Churchmen of the south and began undermining the Arian kingdoms. This partisanship was voiced none-too-subtly by one southern bishop, Avitus of Vienne, in a warm letter congratulating Clovis on his baptism. "Your faith is our triumph," declared Avitus. "Every battle you fight is a victory for us."

In the name of the Faith, Clovis invaded the Visigothic kingdom in 507, and the southern bishops helped him enough to speed Frankish victories. The two armies collided near Poitiers and here Clovis broke the back of Visigothic power in Gaul. Pressing this victory, Clovis marched far to the south, driving most of the Visigoths out of Gaul into Spain. Those vanquished Arians who wished to remain in their former kingdom were permitted to do so under one precedent-setting condition: they had to accept baptism in the Catholic religion. In a few years, the Frankish military and the Frankish Church were joint masters of the vital heartland of the West. Clovis then returned north enriched with Arian booty and very much the Catholic hero (though there is no indication that his spiritual life or moral character had been improved by conversion). He celebrated his success by establishing his capital in a brilliant new location— Paris.

In the next half century, the Merovingian kings and Catholic bishops worked closely together, to their mutual benefit. Then, after Clovis' death in 511, his kingdom was divided among his four sons according to a naïve Frankish custom that would for centuries to come trigger fratricidal warfare in almost every generation. Despite the brutality of Merovingian internecine strife (Clovis' son burned

A PRIMITIVE CHRIST IMAGE, *with a crosslike halo surrounded by animal motifs, stands between two other sacred figures on this reliquary casket that combines pagan vigor with Christian forms.*

one of his rebellious offspring alive), the Frankish realm expanded vigorously: by 534 it included the territory of the Burgundians in southeastern Gaul and, in Germany, the domains of the Alemans and Thuringians. These conquests and the kings' patronage brought endless rewards to the Frankish Church. It was exempted from some taxes and accorded the right to claim taxes and tithes of its own. More important, it received vast gifts of property from noblemen and especially from the kings —this in an age when land was the only real source of wealth. By the beginning of the Eighth Century, the Frankish Church would own an estimated one third of all the land in the realm.

The rapid growth of the Frankish kingdom could not be sustained. By the end of the Sixth Century, conquest had ceased and the decay of the realm had begun. Every level of society was adversely affected, starting at the top. The long-haired kings lost their combative vitality and entered a long decline. Through this period, the family history of the Merovingians was a dismal catalogue of treachery, murder and mutilation. Even worse, in the absence of fighting kings and purposeful wars, the noblemen drifted off into the provinces and joyfully tyrannized the local populace. Everyone was

a potential victim of lawlessness except, ironically, the kings who permitted it; their thrones were held safe by two very different traditions that reinforced each other. The Franks possessed a unique reverence for royal blood; and the bishops, whether or not they remained personally loyal to the kings, were committed by Church policy to support legal process and the duly constituted monarch.

The Frankish Church itself was too deeply involved in this ailing society to avoid contracting its diseases. Incompetence, venality, even immorality infected much of the clergy—an inevitable consequence of corruption in the appointment of bishops. Theoretically a bishop was elected in a regional church council and approved by the people of his district. But the rich episcopal sees now became political plums that the kings could pluck for their favorite courtiers or sell to ambitious aristocrats. Frankish noblemen entered the Church in increasing numbers. Most of them were coarse semiliterates who knew little of Christian doctrine, tradition or liturgy. Some were greedy, willful and nepotistic in the exercise of their enormous powers.

Fortunately for the West, the Church possessed remarkable powers of self-regeneration; and the moral decline of the Frankish clergy was offset by a new source of Christian leadership: the monastery. Vigorous communities of monks multiplied and carried the Faith well beyond the former borders of the Western Roman Empire. Christian monasticism was not a new institution; it had originated in the East in the Fourth Century, and was well established in the West before the collapse of Roman rule. The disintegration of the Roman West was itself a potent stimulus to monastic development. More and more men of piety and principle found it impossible to tolerate the evils of Roman society or the violence that marked the barbarian takeover. These fervent idealists renounced the world for the wilderness. Living alone or among like-minded fellows, they devoted themselves to a harsh regimen of prayer, fasting and meditation.

The most distinguished Western exponents of this tradition were the zealous Celtic monks of Ireland. Many Irish clerics went abroad late in the Sixth Century, established monasteries in Scotland and in the eastern Frankish kingdom, and preached the Faith to the pagans. These monks were well educated and outspoken, and the Frankish bishops had good reason to consider them a threat to their own authority and prestige.

By the middle of the Seventh Century, when the expansion of the Irish monks reached its peak, their monastic tradition was doomed by a new, more temperate and efficient rival. For Western monasticism as it is now known was born in Italy around 529. Its father, the saintly aristocrat Benedict of Nursia, was then just another pious hermit in the Apennine hills east of Rome. From his personal experience, Benedict concluded that only the perfect ascetic was suited to the eremitic life; others, hard put to discipline themselves, seemed to need a firmly organized environment. Benedict led a handful of disciples to a lonely hilltop between Rome and Naples, Monte Cassino, and there he founded a monastery that operated on a fully cenobitic, or communal, basis. For the monks' ready reference, Benedict set down his program and ideals in a remarkable document that he called "A little rule for beginners."

St. Benedict's Rule was the first great practical creation of the post-Roman West. In an age when even simple local institutions (such as the law courts) were notoriously makeshift and ineffective, the Rule blueprinted a complete social system that actually worked. Every monastery was self-sufficient. The monks were required to follow a balanced daily routine of prayer and manual labor; through their work as farmers and craftsmen they supplied all their meager needs by themselves and by trading surpluses with others. The organization of the monastery provided independence and permanence. The monks elected their own governing abbot, whose only superior was to be the pope, and they submitted to the abbot's decisions in all matters, mundane and spiritual. To insure the stability of each little commonwealth, a new pledge was required of the monks. In addition to their classic vows of poverty, chastity and obedience, they swore to remain within the monastery until death, unless specifically given permission to leave.

In spite of the efficacy of the Rule, the Benedictine system very nearly died aborning. Of the early monasteries founded by St. Benedict's disciples, only one or two escaped destruction during the decades of warfare in the later Sixth Century. Yet, paradoxically, it was destruction—the sack of Benedict's original house by the Lombards—that spurred the widespread dissemination of the Rule. Upon fleeing the Lombard marauders around 580, monks from Monte Cassino re-established their community in Rome. Many Roman churchmen were impressed by the Rule. Foremost among them was a monk who later used the Rule as a powerful instrument of international policy—Pope Gregory I, to be known as St. Gregory the Great.

When Gregory was raised to the Holy See in 590, it did not seem likely that his pontificate would be an epoch-making one. Gregory, then in his fiftieth year, was balding and frail; he suffered from a variety of debilitating ailments. Besides, Gregory hardly seemed to fit the conventional picture of a charismatic leader for difficult times. He was gentle in manner and retained the humble bearing of a Benedictine monk. The personality of his reign seemed to be forecast by the papal title he valued most: "servant of the servants of God."

Appearances notwithstanding, Gregory was strong willed, bold and endlessly energetic—and he possessed the very background that could serve the papacy best. The son of an ancient and affluent senatorial family, Gregory had been reared in the great Roman administrative tradition, and he had acquired a wealth of political experience during an illustrious early career in the municipal government of Rome. Gregory had been serving as Rome's highest civil official, prefect of the city, when suddenly, at the age of 33, he resigned his worldly work, gave his fortune to the Church and the poor, and took holy orders in St. Andrew's, a monastery he founded in his former palace in Rome. Gregory's talents were too valuable to be left unused in a cloister for long. He was pressed into service as a deacon of Rome, then sent as a papal envoy to Constantinople. In 590, the self-effacing functionary was back in St. Andrew's as abbot when a virulent plague carried off Pope Pelagius II, and Gregory was elected pontiff by acclaim—despite his earnest protest against serving in the world again.

Gregory's reluctance was routed by responsibility, and his foresighted policies were quickly shaped by developments in Italy. The Lombards, who had been advancing from the Italian north since 568, posed a more or less constant threat to Rome. In 593 Gregory himself was forced to deliver tribute to save the city from attack—an act for which he ruefully called himself "the paymaster of the Lombards." The barbarians, however, also served as a kind of counterpoise to the troops of the Eastern Empire, which still held most of the peninsula to the south of Rome. This precarious balance, which Gregory's diplomacy helped to preserve, gave him a measure of independence from both the Lombard king and the Byzantine emperor and permitted him to follow his keen political intuitions. He recognized that the once-monolithic Roman world was now two distinct cultural blocs, East and West. He continued to claim papal primacy in the East, but he concentrated his efforts on two great tasks in the West: the conversion of the pagan barbarians and the strengthening and reform of the regional churches by unifying them under direct papal control. Largely through Gregory's tireless devotion to these goals, the foundations were laid for the rise of papal power in mundane affairs, and the Church took on its truly international character.

In order to increase papal authority, Gregory involved himself in every aspect of Church affairs and made his presence felt in every Germanic kingdom. He carefully nurtured a growing Catholic minority among the Lombards. In Spain, the baptism of the Arian Visigothic king started the rapid conversion of his people. In a barrage of letters, Gregory lectured king and bishop alike on their abundant shortcomings, especially in moral standards. He even scolded the enlightened Bishop of Vienne for teaching such "idle vanities" as the works of the pagan poets of Classical times. Everywhere Gregory closely identified the papacy with the cause of Church reform.

Of all Gregory's projects, the one that returned the richest dividends started out with the poorest promise. It was a mission to the heathen wilderness of Anglo-Saxon England. If we are to believe a suspiciously attractive anecdote, Gregory's interest in converting the Anglo-Saxons commenced when he saw some blond, fair-skinned captives of war on sale in a slave market in Rome. Upon being told that these comely wretches were Angles, Gregory exclaimed, "Well are they so called, for they have an angel's face, and it is meet that such men were inheritors with the angels in heaven." Whether the tale be factual or fictitious, Gregory fulfilled a long-standing ambition when, in 596, he dispatched to England a small band of Benedictine monks under the leadership of Augustine, an able member of Gregory's own St. Andrew's monastery. As the monks made their way across Gaul, they heard another kind of tale about the alleged "angels"—that they drank human blood and especially enjoyed the Christian variety. This bit of folklore sent Augustine hurrying home to Gregory to recommend the cancellation of the mission. The pope listened to him patiently but was adamant.

Augustine and his party finally landed in England in 597; and—without losing a single drop of blood—they quickly won an important convert in a way that was already familiar. Ethelbert, king of the southeastern realm of Kent, had already indicated his Christian susceptibilities by marrying a pious Frankish princess; his baptism followed —and promptly opened many doors. Thanks to Ethelbert's support, the Italian missionaries were permitted to preach and build churches not only in the district of Kent but also in several other pocket-sized Anglo-Saxon kingdoms that acknowledged Kent's overlordship. Augustine established his seat in Canterbury, and he was ordained the first bishop of the English.

Still another royal mixed marriage gave the missionaries their second major base, this one in northern England. Edwin of Northumbria chose for his queen Ethelbert's Christian daughter; she dowered her groom with her lanky Italian chaplain, Paulinus, whom Pope Gregory had sent as an articulate spokesman for the Christian cause. King Edwin,

Paulinus found, was amenable to conversion—but cautious. In order to test the efficacy of the new faith, Edwin made his baptism contingent on success in his impending attack on the realm of Wessex. The king won a victory, then called a council to win over his followers. The chieftain and his council heard out the Italian monk and succumbed to one of the most potent weapons in the missionary's arsenal—Christian assurances of the afterlife. Soon after this wholesale conversion, Paulinus was ordained archbishop of York.

From the sees of Canterbury and York, a fragile network of missions and churches steadily spread over the southern half of England, and by the end of the Seventh Century most Anglo-Saxons had become Christians. This spiritual conquest did not proceed entirely smoothly, and the missionaries were not denied a fair chance to overcome adversities. In each of England's tiny kingdoms, Christianity was at first not much stronger than the sword arm of its royal protector, and the death or defeat of a baptized king often gave paganism a new lease on life. But the last real obstacle to Christian success was a conflict in the Christian ranks. Redoubtable monks from Ireland were preaching in parts of England, especially in Northumbria. The foot-loose Irishmen and the transplanted Italians engaged in a tug-of-war for converts and, ultimately, for Church jurisdiction in England. The struggle impaired the work of both—and spread confusion among the Anglo-Saxons.

To settle the dispute, King Oswiu of Northumbria called a grand conference at Whitby in 663. Here the rivals staked the future on their small but crucial disagreement over the date of Easter, which the Irish determined according to an old dating formula. Less important to King Oswiu than the merits of either side's argument was his knowledge that the independent Irish possessed not a single worthwhile ally, royal or ecclesiastical; the

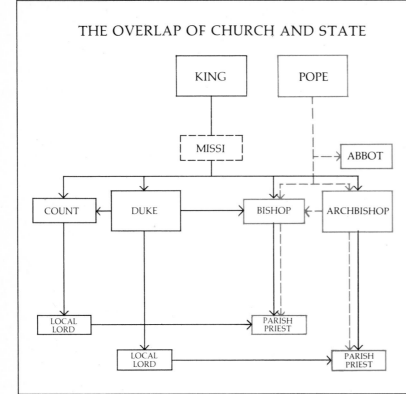

THE OVERLAP OF CHURCH AND STATE

KING

POPE

MISSI

ABBOT

COUNT — DUKE — BISHOP ← ARCHBISHOP

LOCAL LORD

PARISH PRIEST

LOCAL LORD

PARISH PRIEST

This chart shows, in simplified form, the structure of government in much of Europe toward the close of the Eighth Century. With various modifications, the pattern persisted for about 300 years, although power sometimes shifted to a lower administrative echelon during the reign of a weak king.

The authority of the king (black arrows) flowed down through two channels, temporal and ecclesiastical. Overseeing the performances of both state and Church officials were royal inspectors known as "missi."

Dukes and counts, assisted by local lords, were charged with administering the king's justice, collecting his revenues and raising his troops. On the ecclesiastical side archbishops and bishops supervised the parish priests, who were usually appointed by the lords. Although consecrated by the Church, the high-ranking clerics were by and large the king's men; papal authority over them (colored arrows) was limited to matters pertaining to doctrine and to Church affairs.

Italians, on the other hand, were backed by the pope, whose doctrinal authority was freely admitted even by the Irishmen. The decision of Oswiu and the synod in favor of the Italians sealed a momentous victory for the papacy and for Church unity—and it led quickly to others.

By the end of the Seventh Century, Rome's English daughter Church was dispatching groups of well-educated Anglo-Saxon monks on a reverse Christian invasion of the Continent. These monks made especially effective missionaries for several reasons. As newcomers to the Faith themselves, they communicated a fresh, deeply personal, religious enthusiasm to all who heard them preach. Their energies were brought to focus by a leader who was probably the most gifted churchmen to appear between the death of Gregory the Great in 604 and the election of Pope Gregory VII in 1073.

This great English monk was Winfrith of Wessex, renowned and sainted under his Latin name, Boniface. Emerging from an English cloister in 716, at the age of 40, Boniface began his missionary career on Europe's North Sea coast. Christianity east of the Rhine had languished as a semipagan cult until Irish monks arrived to preach, late in the Sixth Century; but the Irishmen, here as in England, lacked resources and organizational strength. Boniface lacked neither. He sent an appeal for help to the English Church, and was answered by a steady influx of eager Benedictines. From the Rhine, bands of black-robed Benedictines fanned out to the east and south, founding monastic outposts as they advanced. Chief among the new houses was Boniface's favorite, Fulda, whose population reportedly rose to 4,000 monks soon after it was founded. Boniface and his brothers converted thousands of Thuringians, Bavarians and other Germans. The pope, recognizing Boniface's accomplishments, made him an archbishop in 732 and assigned him the task of organizing the Church of Germany—that is, the eastern Frankish Church.

While forming the new Church, Boniface worked diligently toward his constant goal—Church reform and the implementation of papal authority. He required his bishops to swear complete obedience to Rome; and one by one the Irish monasteries on the Continent were made to conform with Benedictine standards. By the end of the Eighth Century, the monks of St. Benedict were well on their way to becoming the West's universal monastic order.

While Boniface was pressing Church reforms in the interest of the popes, a rough-and-ready nobleman was starting comparable reforms in the secular leadership of the Frankish kingdom. He began, and his descendants continued, conquests that, by the end of the Eighth Century, would double the size of the Frankish realm and greatly improve the quality of its government. Indeed, their dynamic rule would dominate most of Europe and revitalize its society for almost two centuries.

The man who began these epoch-making changes was Charles Martel, whose surname, meaning "The Hammer," was a tribute to his military success. He belonged to a formidable noble family later called Carolingian after its mightiest scion, Carolus Magnus, or Charles the Great—Charlemagne. In the second half of the Seventh Century, the Carolingians had established their sole hereditary right to the post of mayor of the palace, whose main function was to manage the royal estates. This they had done in a time of utter Merovingian decline. After the death of King Dagobert in 638, the descendants of the ferocious Clovis had petered out into a succession of short-lived weaklings.

Charles, on the other hand, was a hard-headed realist and a tireless organizer. He cooperated with Boniface mainly because the old churchman and his monks were so effective as consolidators of Frankish power beyond the Rhine. But Charles had little interest in him as a papal representative and little time or instinct for the refinements of his diplomacy. He had to fight many hard battles in widely separated places to keep intractable Frankish noblemen in line. And he faced a mounting threat in the form of hostile raiders from Spain, who, by the early 730s, were ranging as far north as the Loire River.

These raiders were Arab Muslims—exponents of the militant faith of Islam. Their invasion of Spain in 711 climaxed a century of conquest in which they had forged a vast empire stretching from India to Africa's Atlantic coast. On landing in Spain, the Muslims crushed the Visigoths in a single decisive battle, and Spain passed out of the Western mainstream for the duration of the Early Middle Ages.

Though the Muslim conquest of Spain was a loss for the West, it had a number of beneficial side-effects. It gave new meaning and solidarity to the concept of Christendom, for Christians everywhere—even traditional enemies—were drawn together by their fear of the so-called "infidels." Moreover, the Frankish kingdom was propelled into the lead in the West in its own self-defense—and with Charles Martel at its helm.

Charles mobilized the realm with brilliance and ruthless dispatch. He even dared to confiscate many Church-owned properties, which he used to bribe or reward Frankish fighting men. In 732, Charles and his host intercepted and mauled a large Muslim force near the towns of Tours and Poitiers. In the hindsight of history, this battle decided little: the Muslims continued to harass the Frankish kingdom for almost two decades before they were driven back and held south of the Pyrenees. But to contemporaries, Poitiers was a providential victory for the Faith; it made Charles a Christian hero and the strongest man in the West.

Charles was now king of the Franks in everything but name, yet he could not claim that empty but infinitely desirable title. By Frankish definition, the king was a Merovingian, and no means existed—in law, in tradition or in Charles' imagination—to separate the title from the royal family. It remained for Charles' son Pepin to find a way to legitimize Carolingian rule.

Pepin was not quite the general his father had been, but he was twice the politician. He proved his acumen as early as 741 by inviting Boniface to reform the corrupt western Frankish Church. The request alone raised Pepin's stock with the pope, and the actual reforms reinforced Pepin's secular authority by disciplining many bishops.

Pepin saw, in his warm and deepening relations with Rome, a possible solution to the kingship problem. In 751, he moved to supersede the Frankish tradition of royal descent by enlisting the help of the supreme authority on divine law, the pope. With the aid of Boniface, if not at his suggestion, Pepin transmitted to Rome a loaded question for Pope Zacharias. Pepin asked, should one man hold the title of king when another man held the power?

This question presented Pope Zacharias with an opportunity ardently hoped for by every pontiff since Gregory the Great. Zacharias now had a chance to seal an alliance between the papacy and the Frankish monarchy—albeit a brand-new Frankish monarchy. By giving Pepin the reply he desired, the pope would make a political debtor of the most powerful man in the West—and this at a time when the Lombards were once again threatening Rome. What was more, Zacharias could oblige Pepin in good conscience, for the Church traditionally had held that temporal authority should be vested only in those entitled to it by their ability and conduct. Pepin had already proven his fitness as a strong, just ruler; he was also suitably reverent and respectable in his private life.

So Zacharias' answer to Pepin declared: "It is better that he who possesses power be called king than he who has none."

Pepin, armed with papal justification, promptly convened the great nobles of the realm and got himself "elected" king of the Franks. The last of the Merovingians, an obscure creature named Childeric III, was symbolically shorn of his long kingly locks and clapped into a monastery. There he considerately died within a year.

King Pepin was duly grateful for the papal endorsement, and he paid his political debt by rescuing the pope from the Lombard threat in two brisk military campaigns. For the papacy, the ultimate reward was to be the success of the Carolingians, and Pope Stephen II, successor to Zacharias, spared no effort to strengthen their rule. His greatest gift to Pepin was a ceremony that established in the West the concept of sacred kingship. This rite, performed first by the ancient Boniface and later by Stephen himself, reached its solemn climax as Pepin was anointed with holy oil in the manner of an Old Testament king. Pepin became king "by the grace of God," and he ruled, moreover, under papal sanctions of awesome power. The Franks were forever forbidden, under peril of excommunication, to choose a king from any family but the Carolingians; revolt against their kingly authority was to be construed as a sin as well as a crime.

However, sanctified kingship was very definitely a two-way street, and, as such, it represented a tremendous advance over tribal kingship. The Merovingians had viewed the entire realm as their personal property, with customary law their sole restraint. Now it was incumbent on the Carolingians to uphold law and justice, to protect the Church, to defend and advance the Faith, and generally to rule in accord with Christian precepts. Such were the duties that Pepin acknowledged and sincerely undertook when he declared, "To us the Lord hath entrusted the care of government."

In many ways the sanctification of Pepin capped and summarized the Church's work of reconstruction in the first three centuries of the post-Roman West. The ceremony, climaxing a legal and peaceful transfer of power, had created a responsible, secular authority—the greatest that the West had known since the death of Emperor Theodosius in 395. To be sure, human frailties would bring many reverses and, as ever, great discrepancies between ideals and practice. But the Christian ethic had been grafted onto barbarian rule, and it would never again be wholly absent from government in the West.

AN ISLAND'S FAITH TRACED IN STONE

One of the brightest lights burning in the darkness of Europe during the Early Middle Ages was the Irish Church. In a time when the Roman Empire had given way to impermanent barbarian states, when scholarship was dim and when Christianity tended to withdraw into its own sanctuaries, Ireland had a Church that was powerful, brilliant and outreaching.

Ireland had remained free from the grasp of Imperial Rome: the distant island beyond the Irish Sea was peopled by fiercely independent tribesmen who had never answered to anyone but local chieftains. After St. Patrick and other Christian missionaries arrived in Ireland in the Fifth Century and until the ultimate Viking destructions of the 10th Century, a distinctly regional church evolved, rooted more in the traditions of the land than in the foreign practices of the early Christians.

The most vivid reminders of that splendid moment of Irish Christianity are carved stone crosses. A detail from the 10th Century Cross of Muirdach *(right)*—with the "Hand of God" overlaying a heathen sun disc and emerging from an interlacing pattern of serpents and saints—demonstrates the lively mixture of pious faith and tradition that characterized Irish Christians.

Photographs by Evelyn Hofer

A Meeting Ground
of Pagan and Christian

On a gray and windswept burial ground in what is now County Kerry stand two related but strikingly different monuments. Their similarities and contrasts demonstrate the slow and peaceful way that Celtic paganism fused into Christianity.

The simple slab at right is a monument to a long-forgotten Celt, who died some 1,500 years ago. He might have been a king, but he certainly was unlettered: his name is indicated on his memorial stone in the primitive symbols called ogham, consisting merely of varying combinations of from one to five strokes, probably derived from a finger language.

The cross at left is a monument to a Christian soul. Like the pagans, the Christian converts of Ireland erected memorials to the dead—stone pillars and several kinds of tablets marked with crosses—whose design reflected both the new Christian belief and the atavistic desire of the people to set up stone monuments against the sky.

The Emerging Celtic Cross

Ireland's converted pagans accepted a new faith but not a new culture. Gradually a pattern of living arose that was both Christian and strongly traditional. The oldest of the early crosses pictured above, the simple pillar at far left, shows a cross growing out of the ground and inscribed in a circle—the

circle being an ancient symbol that in heathen times may have represented the sun. The cross looks curiously like a shamrock. The large cross at center is also linked with a circle; indeed the circle became an integral part of the more sophisticated Irish crosses of the Ninth and Tenth Centuries. And though the cross at right comes from that period when medieval Irish Christianity was reaching its height, it is nonetheless ornamented with monstrous heads that recall the pagans' concept of a spirit-filled world. In Ireland, the old pagan designs and way of life were not destroyed; they were baptized.

A Vivid Banner of Faith

Before Ireland's conversion to Christianity in the Fifth Century there had been little communication between the island-bound Celts and the continent. But eventually the Christians of Ireland began establishing contact with communities of fellow-believers in Europe. A manifestation of this enrichment was the development of the pictorial, free-standing high cross—at left is the central section of one such high cross. It is unstintingly Irish in its preservation of the old Celtic circle and abstract border ornamentation. But it also bespeaks all medieval Christendom as it is predominantly concerned with the Bible. The instructional scenes on both sides of the cross were inspired by a wealth of foreign art forms: Carolingian ivories, Italian icons, Byzantine plates, reliquaries from the Holy Land, even Coptic manuscripts. Particularly popular with sculptors of the Irish crosses were depictions of Christ between sponge and lance-bearers *(center)* and Abraham with his son Isaac *(at right)*.

The Standard Bearer for the Monastery

The High Cross of the Scriptures at Clonmacnoise *(right)* stands today among the deserted ruins of the old monastery. It was erected by an abbot to mark the grave of a king, and thus represents the intertwined and interdependent relationship between the monasteries and Ireland's ancient power structure. Many of the abbots were sons of aristocratic families who remained as mighty in monastic times as they had been in the Celtic kingdoms. From the elaborate monasteries that were established across the land from the Sixth to the Tenth Centuries, these abbots held sway over their self-sustaining communities and parishes. With its sprawling settlement of church, refectory, school, guest quarters and monks' cells, the monastery at Clonmacnoise, like many other famous monastic centers, was not only a source of religious instruction for the land, but also an important place of secular learning with great scholars and artists in residence—its sign the intricate, varied stone cross.

The Monks of Ireland Go Forth

Carved in granite, the tall Moone Cross near the monastery of Castledermot is the tallest of Ireland's Eighth Century crosses. The old pagan and Christian motifs on its west face *(above, left)* are still sharp and evocative—the twelve apostles and Crucifixion on the base, the odd collection of beasts on

the shaft and the whirling demons at the axis of the cross. But on another side of the base is a detail showing the Holy Family's flight into Egypt *(above, right)*, which had a special pertinence to Ireland's missionary monks. They too went into exile in distant lands at God's behest, and viewed separation from their country and family as a form of penitential pilgrimage called "white martyrdom." But in so doing, they spread Christianity from West to East and brought to the barbarian lands of Europe a deep devotion to religious and secular scholarship and a stubborn commitment to the rule of the Cross.

The Cross Unvanquished

Although Ireland had long evaded foreign domination, it could not escape the Vikings, who were attracted to its shores by the wealth of its great monasteries. In the two centuries that followed the first attacks, the "black and white foreigners" (as the Irish called the Norwegians and Danes) stormed through the land.

Ireland at the time was divided into many regions. Thus no united front could be held against the invaders. Nonetheless, many monastic communities survived the Northmen and rebuilt, like the community of Iona, which was relocated at Kells, an ancient stronghold in eastern Ireland. But its unfinished cross *(right)*, with its roughly hewn center panel showing Christ Crucified, serves as a reminder of the Vikings' intrusion and of the Irish monasteries' subsequent decline. With the final Viking defeat in 1014, the golden age of the high crosses ended; thereafter Christianity in Ireland never again represented itself so exuberantly and flamboyantly.

4

BONDS OF CUSTOM

In 1092, Pope Urban II felt obliged to chastise the Count of Flanders for unchristian acts. In his letter of reprimand, the pontiff anticipated the count's defense and neatly rebutted it. "Dost thou claim," wrote Urban with a tinge of sarcasm, "to have done hitherto only what is in conformity with the ancient custom of the land? Thou shouldst know, notwithstanding, thy Creator hath said: My name is Truth. He hath not said: My name is Custom."

The pope's attack on custom was well aimed. Custom did call the tune in medieval times, and it would continue to do so for centuries after Urban's time. Everywhere in the West, obedience to tradition and convention was an instinct, a standard for conduct, an elaborate ritual. This faithfulness to the past held a medieval community together. Yet the dictates of custom and the grim realities of life formed a vicious circle. The meager self-sufficiency of each farming settlement, the difficulty and perils of travel, the deterioration of commerce and currency—such factors tended to break up the West into many minor worlds that hemmed in their natives, closed their borders to outsiders and restricted the interchange of ideas. In each of these isolated agrarian worlds, the people clung almost desperately to every shred of their sparse inheritance of law and religion; it was all they had to add form, color and significance to their drab lives of toil. In turn, their rigid adherence to custom made change of any sort all the more difficult and perpetuated their depressing insularity.

Nevertheless, customs did change—slowly, subtly, but profoundly. Medieval society was itself the product of these and other changes. It was something essentially new—a mixture of Germanic, Roman and Christian cultural elements, all modified in the process of combination. In the second half of the Ninth Century, a variety of traditions from the three cultures would crystallize into the feudal system. But long before feudalism matured, these traditions had decisively changed the character and course of Western civilization.

Medieval government was a ramshackle affair that grew out of Germanic tribal ties of kinship and personal loyalty. By the end of the Sixth Century, this Germanic-style rule had everywhere replaced the Roman administrative system. Just as the

MEDIEVAL LAWGIVERS—*a man representing secular law, a woman, the Church —are depicted in a page from a Ninth Century Frankish manuscript containing several tribal legal codes. Above the figures, the hands with outstretched fingers may stand for the hands of God, the supreme arbiter.*

early conquering Germanic kings had rewarded faithful chieftains with big grants of land, so their medieval descendants rewarded the loyalty of ambitious men by appointing them to the post of count, to act as royal agents in outlying districts, or counties. The counts were sworn to fidelity and charged with three main tasks: to raise troops for the royal army; to collect revenues due the king (a portion of which was theirs to keep for expenses or for their trouble); and, most important, to serve as the king's representative in the local courts.

Most counts took this delegation of authority as an outright gift of absolute, independent power. Experience proved with monotonous regularity that the ties of an oath of fidelity could not be stretched very far before they snapped. When a new count reached his county, he usually set about to accumulate wealth and hereditary privilege at the expense of the king and everyone else. A strong king might force his embezzling, self-willed counts to toe the line. But a strong king's rule lasted only as long as his lifetime; no barbarian king was able to set up an apparatus of central government capable of sustaining itself through the reign of a weak or inactive successor. With few brief exceptions, each kingdom was really an anomalous series of semidetached regions; political power remained the local monopoly of the counts and a land-rich warrior elite, whose rule differed greatly from place to place and from generation to generation.

Though the counts were usurpers and government was a shambles, this disorganized state of affairs was probably not considered bad by the medieval masses; to them it was just normal. Under tribal tradition, the people were burdened by even fewer civic responsibilities than was the king, and certainly the peasants had no reason to identify their best interests with the monarch. When the king's troops intervened in local affairs they damaged crops and property without accomplishing any measurable good. Besides, the kings did not endear themselves to their subjects by providing much in the way of public services; on the contrary, they allowed the old Roman roads to fall into disrepair, and they even made the royal soldiers outfit themselves out of their own pockets.

Since the people saw little evidence of royal interest or expenditure in their behalf and since their tribal past was unsullied by taxation, they assumed naturally—and quite correctly—that most taxes represented a flagrant attempt on the king's part to augment his private fortune. Nearly everyone paid the tolls and tariffs demanded by the count in the king's name, and it would have been foolhardy to refuse, with the count's armed henchman on the spot. But the king himself remained a remote, shadowy figure and most people probably wanted from him nothing more than his continued absence, plus his guarantee of their day in the local court presided over by the count.

To the people of medieval times, the law was a prized birthright. It was one of the few relatively stable institutions in an era of violent upheavals; it was a bond maintaining group identification in a day when national loyalty was unknown; and it offered some protection against injustice in a world ruled by naked force.

Law, however, was no simple matter, even for the counts who casually ignored it to suit their own purposes. Medieval law was fundamentally Germanic law; it prevailed everywhere in a bewildering variety of crude barbarian legal codes that both reflected and contributed to the problems of weak, decentralized government. In the preliterate Germanic past, many customary laws had been evolved by tribal groups living under nomadic or seminomadic conditions; these laws, surviving through centuries of oral transmission, had been written down as legal codes after the

Germanic peoples completed their conquests in the West. The multiplicity of codes, and the uncompromising loyalty of each people to its own law, created strange legal tangles for settled societies—tangles that were never wholly cleared away in the Early Middle Ages.

The jurisdiction of each legal code was tribal rather than territorial. For example, a man born of Anglo-Saxon parents was considered an Anglo-Saxon by definition; and as such he was entitled to be judged under Anglo-Saxon law whether he was living in Frankish Gaul or traveling in Visigothic Spain. Under this common Germanic tradition, every local court had to honor the birthright of every individual and try him under his own law. The principle was frequently put to the test, for outlanders were much in evidence despite the hazards of travel. According to a Ninth Century Frankish archbishop: "It often happened that five men were present or sitting together, and not one of them had the same law as another." In the course of a single year a local court might find it necessary to invoke each of about ten barbarian legal codes at one time or another.

Still other difficulties beset legal process. The steady decline of literacy resulted in a paucity of men who could read and write, and hence in a shortage of clerks to record proceedings for future reference. But the severest threat to effective law and stable government came from quite another quarter. It came, ironically, from the most stable and effective social unit of prefeudal times.

That unit was the kindred, a traditional Germanic grouping of families related by blood and marriage. The families of a kin group, which might total 50 to 250 relatives, usually lived in the same community and often fought bitterly among themselves. But each kindred policed the conduct of its members, shared the debts and hardships of a stricken family, and seldom failed to present a solid front to a dangerous world. This unity gave formidable strength to any kin group, whether it consisted of peasants or of royalty. Graphic evidence of the kin's grim solidarity appears in a medieval legal document that uses the old French word *amis*—friends—to define kinsmen. The obvious implication—that friendship seemed possible only among relatives—was borne out all too often in violent feuds between two kindreds.

The blood feud was a venerable Germanic practice that probably did more to disrupt medieval society than anything but the plague. It took very little to start a vendetta in a society of fighting men with hair-trigger tempers. If a man made a slighting remark about another man's courage, the honor of two kindreds might be at stake. Should anyone be slain in an ensuing scuffle, the dead man's relatives were duty bound to take revenge on the killer or on any of his kinsmen. As a forceful reminder of this obligation, the Frisians of the North Sea coast would hang the corpse of a murdered man from the rafters of his home; his relatives could not bury the body until they had killed one of the enemy kin. Once begun, a vendetta tended to escalate and perpetuate itself. Medieval chroniclers have left behind many accounts of blood feuds that decimated rival kindreds for two or three generations; occasionally entire clusters of communities were plunged into anarchy.

How could society preserve itself against its own ancient and honorable traditions of violence? This was the central dilemma that Germanic law was improvised to resolve. Significantly, none of the legal codes was drafted in a systematic effort to cope with the problem in principle or even in a general way. Each consisted of concrete tribal precedents validated by traditional or "customary" use. It was this unpremeditated, collective origin that gave customary law not only its sanctity in the eyes of the people, but its peculiar limitations as well.

The barbarians' codes remained relatively crude until they were superseded by feudal law in the 10th Century. They never drew sharp distinctions between personal injury and civil crime, much less between right and wrong. Nevertheless, the various compilations reveal a resolute practicality and flashes of real ingenuity. More important, they reflect a strong commitment to the idea that law was the possession of the people—a possession to be defended by them and the king alike against all infringements. Also, quite inadvertently, these traditional codes provide a unique insight into medieval society and into the values of the people who were creating it.

Each legal code consisted primarily of a long list of offenses and matching cash fines. The fine, to be paid by the offender, was obviously intended to appease the injured party, thereby stopping a fight or, better yet, settling a grievance before it started a fight. Most of the offenses were of the homely, bucolic sort that might be expected to occur in a society that had become almost entirely rural. The Franks' Salic Law, for example, devoted fully 74 of its 343 articles to the theft of livestock and domestic animals. The penalty for stealing a bull was 45 gold *solidi;* for stealing an ox, 35 *solidi;* for a common farm dog, 15 *solidi.* These were stiff fines in terms of medieval purchasing power. In Italy, for instance, the 15 *solidi* exacted for dog-theft could buy an olive grove, or in Gaul it might purchase a vineyard. The payment of so heavy a fine could even cost the owner of such a property his title to it. By paying a fine, in coin or kind, the criminal terminated his responsibility—and the court's interest in the case. No disciplinary action followed, for in the eyes of the law, the offense had been purely a transgression against the individual, not a crime against God or society.

In cases of homicide, the law's basic attitude was much the same. An injury had been done to the deceased and his kindred, for which a proper penalty must be imposed. The indemnity, to be sure, was a much stiffer one than that for theft; but cash usually sufficed to make amends, and the size of the fine seldom reflected differences in degree of culpability. Indeed, the legal codes showed rather less interest in the motive of a killer than they did in the social rank of his victim.

Class consciousness marked all Germanic law. Under every code, the fines for homicide varied according to the dead man's status, and they were so precisely graduated as to diagram the whole social order. At the bottom of the social ladder was the slave. Slaves were valuable properties; but the fine for killing a slave was the same as for killing a horse. Ranked above the slaves was the class of freemen, lesser churchmen and serfs, who were technically free though economically dependent. Every male in this freeman class had an official life value—called *wergeld* ("man-money")—which had to be paid as a fine in case of his death by homicide. Under Burgundian law, the freeman's *wergeld* was a round and impressive 150 *solidi.* However, men of the upper class, which included noblemen and high clerics, were protected by a death-fine twice as intimidating—300 *solidi.*

At the top of the social ladder stood the royal kindred. In very early times, many tribes had cast a mantle of sanctity over members of royal families, and their status remained supreme in the legal codes despite the vicissitudes of medieval kingship. The slaying of an immediate member of a royal family could usually be indemnified only by the death of the killer. Men in the king's service were also specially protected. Under Frankish law, the fine for killing a royal retainer was triple the dead man's normal *wergeld.*

Each free woman and noble woman was also dignified by a specific *wergeld.* Smaller than a freeman's or a nobleman's to begin with, a female's

COURT AND GALLOWS *are juxtaposed in a manuscript illumination showing the administration of medieval justice. The penalty of death—a punishment meted out for many crimes—has been imposed by a sword-bearing king flanked by a council of advisors.*

life-value was automatically reduced if she married below her station, and it was ungallantly reduced even further if she was slain after childbearing age.

This low value placed on a woman's life reflected the trivial status of all women in that age dominated by warrior males. The first fact of life for every female was that she had few rights of any kind. She could not inherit real estate if any male relative existed or buy and sell valuables on her own volition. Theoretically, the only grounds for divorce were adultery, the practice of witchcraft or the desecration of a tomb or church; but few women dared to institute divorce proceedings, while many husbands nonchalantly discarded their wives on mere whim. Married or unmarried, divorced or widowed, a "free" woman was everywhere forbidden to live according to her own free will; as Lombard law decreed, "she must remain always under the power of men, and if no one else, under the power of the king."

In spite of these built-in social inequalities, the law sought earnestly to be fair, and once a case was brought to court its workings had an awesome inviolability for people of all classes. During the course of a trial, the law proceeded inevitably—almost without human guidance, it seemed—through one or more time-honored procedures until the verdict finally made itself obvious to all and was accepted as an infallible truth—a manifestation of God's will. For this was an age of fierce, superstitious piety. All people believed that God intervened directly in human affairs, and therefore they assumed that the Lord would take a hand in each trial to make the truth known and to protect the innocent from harm. Germanic justice had placed itself hopefully under quasi-Christian auspices.

When the participants in a lawsuit filed into court, they became actors in what was in effect a religious drama. Before them, in impressive array, sat the members of the court: the presiding count or his personal representative; a panel of important local people who acted as advisors; and a number of clerks whose main function was to state legal precedents that pertained to the case. Essentially, the court served merely as referee; there was no judge or jury as we know them today. God was invoked, solemn oaths were administered and the play unfolded.

In most cases the burden of proof rested squarely on the defendant. Once his accuser had vowed that he was guilty, the defendant was obliged to refute the evidence against him, which often included hearsay and pure surmise. He swore his innocence and made his defense in a statement whose form and style were minutely prescribed by ancient custom. If he managed to complete the ritual in good order, it was clear to the court that he had sworn truly. His accuser, if he had deliberately perjured himself while calling upon God to witness the veracity of his charges, faced divine justice in the form of eternal damnation. If the defendant made the slightest slip, however—if he hesitated, coughed or stammered—it was considered a sure sign that God recognized his guilt, and the accused usually lost his case. These indications of guilt or innocence were interpreted by the count or members of the court or occasionally by a Church consultant.

Of course, the defendant's "true" oath might not be enough to exonerate him, for his accuser's oath had also presumably been true. In the absence of conclusive evidence, such as the testimony of an impartial and respected eyewitness, the defendant might bring in "oath-helpers" to swear to the truth of his oath. For practical purposes, however, the verdict might be decided by the oath of a nobleman, for his "swear-worth" was at least six times as great as an ordinary freeman's. But, the law took into full account the individual's char-

acter as well as his swear-worth. An especially notorious Frankish queen had to obtain the oaths of three bishops and 300 noblemen in order to "prove" her sworn word that her son, allegedly illegitimate, had indeed been sired by the king. On the other hand, the universally admired Bishop Gregory of Tours was permitted to clear himself of a slanderous charge of calumny: he had only to swear his innocence at three different altars.

If the testimony of oath-helpers failed to indicate a clear-cut verdict, the defendant could "prove" his innocence unequivocally by submitting to the awesome and infallible test of trial by ordeal. He had many such trials to choose from. All of them were hoary with tradition, and the severity of the one used was determined by the gravity of the offense. The accused could hold his hand in a fire, or walk between blazing piles of wood, or carry a red-hot iron bar, or pick up a stone from the bottom of a cauldron of boiling water. A few days after the ordeal took place, the defendant would be pronounced innocent if his injuries were healing cleanly, guilty if they were infected.

Should the accused be squeamish, he might choose a less painful but potentially more hazardous ordeal—the trial by cold water. In this test, he was bound hand and foot and heaved into a lake or stream. His innocence was established if he sank, and it was unfortunate if he drowned before the court could fish him out. But if he floated too soon, he was certainly guilty, for, as Bishop Hincmar of Rheims explained with unedifying logic, "the pure nature of water recognizes and therefore rejects as inconsistent with itself such human nature as has once been regenerated by the waters of baptism and is again infected by falsehood."

An especially common form of test was trial by battle, or judicial combat. The accuser and the accused fought under oath, and it was assumed that God would award the victory to the man who had

A SYMBOL OF SANCTUARY, *this huge door knocker from England's Durham Cathedral was often used to gain asylum in the Church, a man's last refuge from the harsh sentences of medieval law.*

sworn truly. This assumption, to be sure, was challenged by a few enlightened individuals, mostly churchmen, who declined to attribute to God any legal decision reached through violence. One archbishop, Agobard of Lyons, roundly denounced ordeals in general and judicial combat in particular, declaring, "If in this life the innocent were always the victors and the guilty were vanquished . . . Herod would not have killed John, but John, Herod."

The Church itself, however, had been highly secularized and barbarized by the Seventh Century; although churchmen were exempted from ordeal by battle, many chose that form of trial and availed themselves of the option to be represented by a champion. When judicial combat became the customary method of settling litigation over land, a bishop or an abbot often sent a swordsman into combat to defend or extend the boundaries of an ecclesiastical estate. Many land-rich monasteries kept powerful warriors on retainer to fight their frequent judicial battles. In a rare and startling case, rival groups of clerics in Visigothic Spain actually sent their champions into combat to decide which of two rituals to use in church.

Whatever trial form was used to decide a case, the verdict was bound to be clear-cut. What is

more, it stood a good chance of satisfying both parties and preserving peace. If a trial for homicide ended in acquittal, the decision protected the defendant by absolving the deceased's kinsmen of their duty to take revenge, while a verdict of guilty pacified them financially with the dead man's *wergeld.* The sum of the fine (minus the king's commission, sometimes as much as one third) was divided among the kindred as specified by law. Relatives in the male line of descent (the "spear" side) usually received the larger portion, the remainder going to kin in the female line (the "distaff" side). As for the "guilty" defendant, he might reconcile himself to an adverse verdict even if he was innocent. After all, it was God's will.

But submission to fate never helped a poor man, innocent or otherwise, to pay a heavy fine. Economic ruin became commonplace. Severe fines often forced small free farmers, short of cash, to deed their lands to wealthy noblemen, thereby consigning themselves and their immediate families to the swelling ranks of half-free serfs. Serfs, having already exhausted their negotiable assets, were ordered by the courts to work off a delinquent fine or to suffer any torments that successful litigants might impose in irate impatience. To escape such eventualities, many convicted men fled the community and hid in the forests and hills beyond. Some men lived as solitary exiles and subsisted on what they could scavenge or on game when they could find it. But hunting was itself an offense, for hunting rights were strictly protected as the privilege of the nobility. Other refugees joined robber bands and preyed on travelers. Whether a renegade lived by poaching or by brigandage, he was literally an outlaw: having placed himself beyond the law, he might be cut to pieces or hanged on sight. All in all, the outlaw's life was one of grubby hardship and constant danger; its only charms were imaginary, the invention of bards who began spinning such subversive romances as that of Robin Hood in the 14th or 15th Century.

A man facing an unpayable fine had one escape-route short of outlawry. He could take refuge in the nearest church and claim sanctuary under a tradition that had its roots in remote pagan times. The churchmen interceded for penitent refugees and urged the authorities to temper justice with mercy. Moreover, these appeals were often heeded.

Clerical efforts in behalf of convicted men were only one of many ways in which churchmen began to moderate the more barbaric practices of early medieval society. The beginnings, to be sure, were small and slow; the Church, being a loose-knit and conservative institution, conducted nothing resembling an organized international campaign for legal reform. All the same, men of the Church were the first to act on moral principle; they asserted Church leadership in doing good works and setting precedents for civil responsibility. Bishop Felix of Nantes built levees against the flooding of the Loire River, and a bishop of Mainz dammed the Rhine. Other bishops and abbots built hospitals and orphanages as church annexes. Many churchmen—and churchmen alone—dispensed charity on a regular basis, giving to the destitute monthly allotments of money and supplying them with produce from ecclesiastical estates.

The practice of slavery began to decline partly because of clerical pressure. Here the power and the ambiguity of the Church's role were equally clear. The Church officially condoned slavery: the canon law of the Church recognized slaves as one of three basic social classes (the others being clergy and freemen), and some lordly clerics were themselves slaveowners. Nevertheless, Church doctrine held that all men were equal in the eyes of God, and slaves were accorded the right to receive the sacraments along with everyone else. In keeping with this spirit, humane churchmen commended the manumission of slaves as an act of piety. The response was hardly overwhelming, but rich noblemen did free an occasional human chattel in the hopes of improving their chances in the hereafter. Sometimes the act of manumission was actually performed as a religious ceremony in church. In Lombard Italy, where the freeing of a slave was an involved legal procedure, the climax came when the slave was escorted to a crossroads, handed an arrow as the emblem of freedom, and then told in the presence of witnesses, "You may take whichever of these four roads you will, you have free power." No matter what road the freed slaves might choose, it would almost always lead them to a half-free serfdom—a small gain for liberty, but a gain nonetheless.

Even as Christian influences were beginning to stabilize and ameliorate society, Christian practices were themselves being changed by customs carried over from earlier times. The cause of these changes was the limited understanding of illiterate peoples. It took the Church centuries of patient labor to teach the true meaning of the Faith and bring the religious practices of its congregants into accord with Christian belief.

The problem of religious indoctrination had been a frustrating one for the Church since the first Germanic barbarians were baptized. While those superstitious warriors eagerly embraced Christianity as a superior cult, many of them also clung to their traditional pagan war-gods and nature-spirits. Zealous churchmen found that it did little good to destroy pagan shrines. The new Faith and the old one tended to coexist, and were practiced alternately or simultaneously. This informal arrangement became the key to official Church policy during the pontificate of Gregory the Great (590-604). That practical and far-sighted pope likened Christianity to a steep mountain that had to be climbed step by step, not in a single leap, and he

A CURIOUS SHRINE, *containing a sandal of St. Andrew, was among count-less reliquaries made in medieval times to hold a saint's remains or an object associated with him. This jewel-encrusted and ivory-paneled piece, from the Cathedral of Trier, could also be utilized as a portable altar.*

instructed his missionaries to desist from their efforts to obliterate ancient pagan customs "of a sudden." Instead, he said, they were to infuse heathen practices with Christian meaning and to adapt pagan temples to the worship of the True God. This policy slowly transferred local religious loyalties to the Church, and assured the continuing growth and vigor of Christianity.

The result was popular or "folk" religion—a lively blend of Christianized pagan survivals and barbarized Christian practices. The religious synthesis produced a number of colorful festivals. The pagan celebration of Midsummer's Night became part of the feast of St. John's Day, with the exorcism of demons remaining a prominent feature. Christ's birthday was celebrated on December 25, coinciding with the pagan festival of the winter solstice, and it became a popular folk holiday. The year's work was done; the cattle that could not be fed through the hard northern winters had been slaughtered; and families had leisure to gather for eating and drinking in such excess as they could afford. For the kings and their courts, Christmas became the convenient and propitious day for holding councils and coronations.

Folk religion centered on the veneration of the saints, a custom begun by the early Christians in Roman times. It thrived on the credulity of the people who clung to the traditions of personalized, intimate worship. Everyone, great and humble alike, believed in magic and miracles, and the fertile medieval imagination transformed belief into reality. Even Bishop Gregory of Tours, one of the best-educated men of the Sixth Century, reported that he was saved from a band of robbers by the intercession of St. Martin, the patron saint of Tours. Prayers to certain saints came to be regarded as especially efficacious for specific purposes or for people of particular occupations. Sailors and fishermen, who had once appealed to pagan sea-gods, addressed their prayers to St. Nicholas, who in life had been a much-traveled Eastern bishop. The martyrdom of the saints replaced the deeds of warriors as the favored subject matter for everyday yarn-spinning in kitchens and barns. And the saints proliferated mightily. Modern scholars have amassed a collection of stories telling of more than 25,000 saints.

The cult of the saints reached a peak of feverish intensity in the veneration of saintly relics. As late as the Fifth Century, this practice had been vigorously opposed by the Church. No less an authority than St. Augustine, Bishop of Hippo in North Africa, declared: "Let us not treat the saints as gods; we do not wish to imitate those pagans who adore the dead." But popular devotion to old customs led to a radical change in Church policy. In 787 a general Church council decreed, "If any bishop from this time forward is found consecrating a temple without holy relics, he shall be deposed as a transgressor of the ecclesiastical traditions." No bishop transgressed. As a network of parish churches spread outward from each episcopal see, magnificent processions were frequently seen winding their way through the countryside, bearing holy remains to the new houses of worship. Inevitably, the supply of relics, many of them flagrant duplications, kept expanding to meet the demand. But in the Early Middle Ages, the authenticity of a relic was irrelevant to the purpose it served: piety, however naïve, was its own reward in a time when so many conditions were beyond man's control. People with desperate causes made arduous pilgrimages, some covering hundreds of miles, to the shrines of great saints. At the end of each hopeful journey was a glittering reliquary containing some revered human fragment.

If any one object epitomized the era, it was the reliquary, not the Cross. Most people had not yet grasped the symbolism of Christ's sacrifice on the Cross; the King of Heaven, like a mundane monarch, was a remote figure. But everyone understood the reliquary; it was representative rather than symbolic, tangible rather than remote. Its shape was often that of the mortal remains it contained—a finger, a foot, a head. The reliquary was worked in the familiar style of barbarian jewelry, crudely fashioned of gold or silver and lavishly studded with gems and colored glass. The total impression was one of power and wealth such as no ordinary man could achieve in this world. These richly wrought images must have confirmed the conviction of every supplicant that his prayers would be answered in life, or, more important, that his faith would be rewarded after death.

Apart from their religious significance, we today may admire reliquaries as works of art. But the essential outlook on life that they expressed remains alien and elusive. In early medieval times, it seems, all things merged or interpenetrated. Heaven and earth overlapped: angels and saints crossed freely back and forth. Government and religion were one: bishops served as secular leaders and kings appointed warriors as bishops. The medieval mind easily reconciled the greatest contradictions. Society was fragmented and turbulent, yet it enjoyed a sense of unity and order in its concept of Christendom.

Underlying these paradoxes was the prosaic fact that medieval civilization was developing in two opposite ways. One trend, toward unity and a common "customary" culture, was represented by the synthesis of diverse Christian, Roman and Germanic elements to form popular religion and medieval law. At the same time, disunity and diversity were on the rise, fostered by increasing distinctions among regions, languages and classes.

Both trends were gaining momentum as the Eighth Century wore on. But it was still uncertain which one would ultimately triumph.

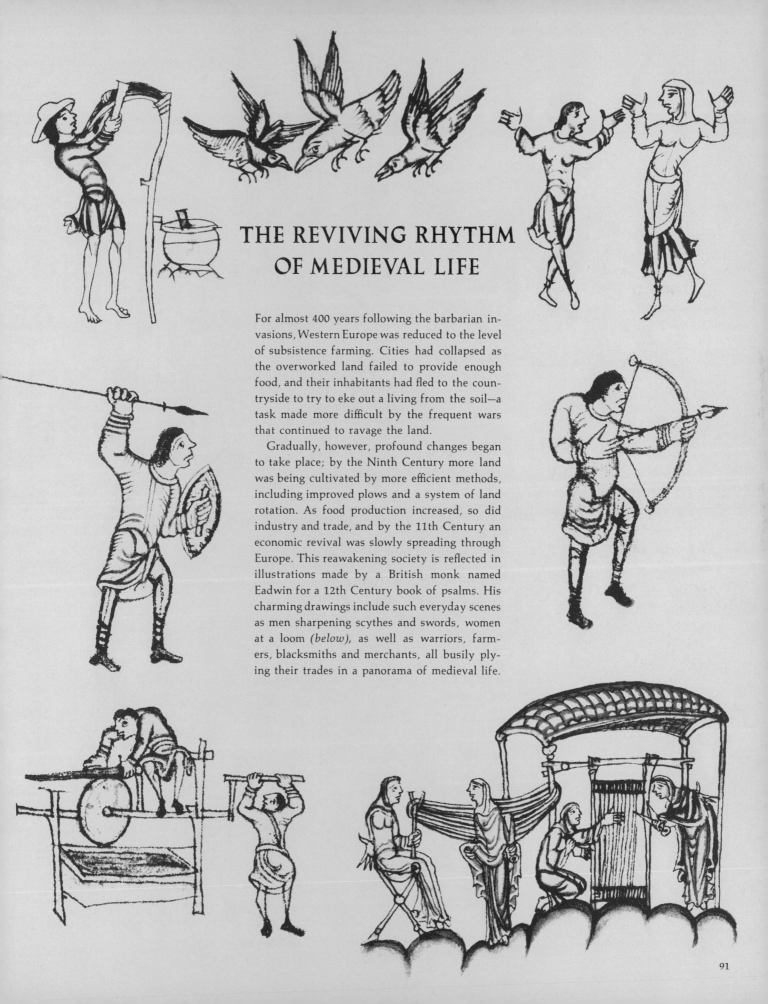

THE REVIVING RHYTHM OF MEDIEVAL LIFE

For almost 400 years following the barbarian invasions, Western Europe was reduced to the level of subsistence farming. Cities had collapsed as the overworked land failed to provide enough food, and their inhabitants had fled to the countryside to try to eke out a living from the soil—a task made more difficult by the frequent wars that continued to ravage the land.

Gradually, however, profound changes began to take place; by the Ninth Century more land was being cultivated by more efficient methods, including improved plows and a system of land rotation. As food production increased, so did industry and trade, and by the 11th Century an economic revival was slowly spreading through Europe. This reawakening society is reflected in illustrations made by a British monk named Eadwin for a 12th Century book of psalms. His charming drawings include such everyday scenes as men sharpening scythes and swords, women at a loom (below), as well as warriors, farmers, blacksmiths and merchants, all busily plying their trades in a panorama of medieval life.

War and Its Weapons

The constant warfare of the Early Middle Ages touched practically all Europeans, disrupting their communities and trade. During the centuries when the Germanic tribes were conquering Roman territories, armies were composed mainly of foot soldiers who fought with spears or bows and arrows *(left)*, or used broad-bladed swords in bloody close-in contests *(above right)*.

In the years that followed, the nature of war changed. Kings fought one another for power and local lords battled among themselves to enlarge their land holdings; both conscripted their peasants as infantry to carry out their will. By the mid-Eighth Century, however, the decisive factor on the battlefield had become cavalry, armed with long spears and battle-axes *(upper left)*. The use of horsemen gave fighting forces greater mobility and power, but even so they were not sufficiently well organized to stop the Viking raids of the Ninth and Tenth Centuries. Striking swiftly before defending troops could arrive, the fierce Scandinavian warriors plundered with virtual impunity, pillaging towns and sacking churches *(above left)*, to make off with their treasures of jeweled caskets and gold plate.

93

Salvation from the Soil

For centuries agriculture had been bound by age-old methods, many of them developed for the climate and light soil of Italy and ill suited for conditions north of the Mediterranean. Beside village walls, like the one shown below, farmers were barely able to scratch the surface of their moist, heavy soil with light plows, and the seed they sowed by hand often blew away, or at best produced only meager, low-quality crops.

In the Ninth and Tenth Centuries, however, Europeans were beginning to benefit from such useful innovations as the nailed iron horseshoe and the horsecollar, as well as heavy, iron-shod plows like the one shown below, which dug deeply into the heavy earth, enabling farmers to prepare better seedbeds and open up new lands to larger crops. The beasts pulling the plow here were sketched, for reasons best known to the artist, with faces that look almost human.

A Rebirth of Commerce

As improved farming began to restore an adequate food supply, trade sprang up and urban life began to revive. By the year 1000, a new class of artisans and tradesmen was forming to serve the needs of a growing population. Quarriers and masons helped erect durable new buildings of stone *(left)*; professional blacksmiths hammered out tools and horseshoes on forges *(right)*; cutlers sharpened swords and plowshares on grindstones like the two-man contraption pictured at center below.

A farmer bringing his produce to market no longer had to rely entirely on barter for an exchange of goods, but could be paid in money; coins, scarce for centuries, were now coming back into general use. Nor were farm products the only commodities at the market; merchants sold such staples of medieval life as bagged salt and cuts of coarse linen *(bottom pictures)*.

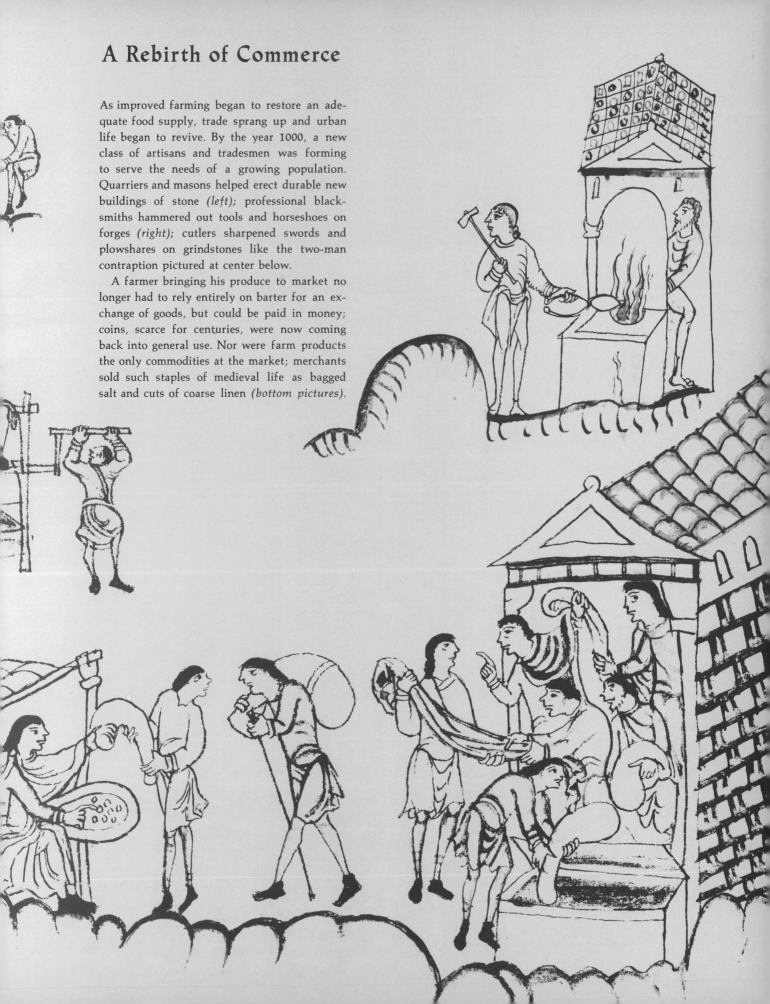

Pleasures of Wealth

For the landed lords in particular, the new prosperity meant a more luxurious way of life. By the 11th Century many were beginning to enjoy the security of stone castles instead of wooden manor houses, and with time to cultivate the pleasures of wealth they increasingly pursued the traditional pastimes of the nobility.

Among their favorite sports was hunting with hounds or falcons *(left and below)*; noblemen jealously guarded their hunting preserves, prohibiting peasants from killing wild boar and other game. In the evenings the lords and their retinues often relaxed at lusty banquets, where they were entertained by musicians *(right)* or amused by performers like those shown at the lower right. This particular gathering was enlivened by a juggler, a horn player and a "dancing" bear—which, in the heat of the festivities, seems to have collapsed from his exertions.

5

CHARLEMAGNE'S EUROPE

In the second half of the Eighth Century, a famous king and a little-used term were connected in the minds of the few clerics who made up the intellectual community of the medieval West. The term was Europe. The king was Charlemagne (meaning Charles the Great), a big, bull-necked, pot-bellied man who inherited the Frankish throne in 768 and ruled with enormous gusto and iron-handed benevolence for 46 years. One contemporary chronicler, looking back on Charlemagne's long reign, alleged that it "had left all Europe in the greatest happiness." Poets praised Charles, describing him as the "chief of Europe" and the "father of Europe."

These tributes to Charlemagne were well deserved. Through his conquests he extended the borders of Western society to include great new areas of the continent. In his efforts to improve government and education he laid the foundations for a common culture that many peoples have been building on ever since. It is no wonder that Charlemagne became a father-figure to the people of medieval Europe. The vast extent of his realm and the firmness of his rule gave men of his time a vague but satisfying sense of belonging to a single great community. "Europe" was only one of the terms they applied to that community, but it was the term that would triumph in the end.

The idea of Europe had been stirring fitfully for more than a millennium before Charlemagne's time —since the Greeks had applied the name of their goddess Europa to the landmass west of the River Don. By the Fifth Century A.D., the Church Fathers had begun to Christianize the pagan term and evolve a geography that related "Europe" to Biblical references to the three sons of Noah. Japheth was designated the first settler of Europe and forefather of the gentiles, while Asia was said to be the homeland of Shem's progeny, the Jews, and Africa the patrimony of Ham's descendants.

This fanciful geography gained in credence after the breakup of the monolithic Roman Empire. By 700, there had emerged a world that was in fact tripartite, but one whose organization differed from that conceived by the Church Fathers. Islam held much of Western Asia and all of North Africa and within a few years would conquer nearly all Spain. Byzantium was temporarily reduced by Muslim successes to a strong defensive heartland centered on Constantinople. By elimination, if not by definition, the rest of the known world was Europe.

Because the growing threat of Islam aroused Christian religious loyalties, the idea of Europe lacked the emotional appeal of another half-formed conception, that of Christendom. Consistent with Christianity's sense of worldwide mission, Christendom was viewed by scholars of the Eighth Century as a spiritual union that neither possessed nor acknowledged territorial boundaries; it existed wherever a single believer professed the Faith. And with the concept of Christendom in command of the Western imagination, the term "Europe" could serve only one purpose for which there was no compelling need—to describe the West in a specifically geographical context. Thus the idea of Europe floated aimlessly, without real political focus or cultural content, until the advent of Charlemagne.

When Charlemagne came to the throne he no doubt was aware of the speculation regarding "Europe"—but such scholarly speculation could have had only secondary interest to a monarch whose overriding concern was the effective use of power. Charlemagne brought to the kingship not only great strength and stamina but also a keen mind and an insatiable desire to learn, and he kept himself exceptionally well informed. However, he valued ideas and learning not so much for their own sake as for the purposes they might serve. Even if he considered Europe while embarking on the conquests that helped to define it, it was probably only as terrain—not as a cultural and political entity.

As a war leader, Charlemagne displayed little of the dash and tactical genius of his grandfather Charles Martel; but he possessed a relentless determination and a rare gift for concentrating his troops at the right place in the nick of time. Over a period of some three decades and on several fronts, he launched 60 major campaigns, half of which he supervised himself—often on two or more fronts at the same time. Driving into what is now Hungary, Charlemagne crushed the Avars, invading nomads from Asia, and, to prevent further Asiatic incursions, set up two marks, or marches— one of which formed the nucleus of medieval Austria. South of the Pyrenees, in Spain, he wrested the county of Barcelona from the Muslims and eventually made himself overlord of the small Christian principalities in the Spanish northeast. It was while Charlemagne was returning home from one of these Spanish campaigns that his rear guard was wiped out in the pass of Roncesvalles by the independent Basques—a calamity that inspired the rousing medieval epic poem, the *Song of Roland.*

Charlemagne invaded Italy very much against his will. He well knew that more could be lost than won in the small wars and involved intrigues chronically embroiling the peninsula's many splinter factions. In 771 the Lombards—as they had so often done in the previous two centuries—again broke treaties wholesale, seizing papal lands and threatening Rome. Charlemagne was committed to honor the Frankish alliance that his father, Pepin, had sealed with the papacy, and by 774 he had defeated the Lombards and occupied Italy almost as far south as Naples. To prevent the Lombards from causing trouble in the future, Charlemagne assumed direct rule as their king.

Charlemagne acted as decisively in his settlement with the papacy as he had with the Lombards. Wary of the steady growth of papal claims to temporal power, he refused to return to Pope Adrian most of the lands that the Lombards had seized, even though Pepin had granted them to Rome under the terms of his so-called Donation of Pepin. Charlemagne treated Adrian and his successor Leo III with great respect and kindness, but he left no doubt in their minds as to who was boss.

Throughout the years of his military operations,

Charlemagne was heavily engaged east of the Rhine River. In a series of campaigns, he ultimately consolidated most of what is now West Germany into a political whole under Frankish rule. He took over complete control of the semiautonomous duchy of Bavaria, which had shown an alarming preference for complete self-rule. The Frisians of the North Sea coast, a sea-going people who for a half-century had resisted the Franks and the Church as one enemy in two guises, finally succumbed to Charlemagne and to a type of conversion that a few high-minded clerics deplored as "baptism with the sword." The king, undismayed by such criticism, applied the policy with even greater fervor in winning his most important victory. After about 30 years of fierce, sporadic warfare, he vanquished and pacified the many small tribes of pagan Saxons in northeastern Germany. On at least one occasion, Charlemagne followed the standard medieval practice of slaughtering captives—4,500 of them; less barbarously and more imaginatively, he neutralized 10,000 intractable Saxon warriors by deporting them to Frankish lands west of the Rhine. The Saxons, backed to the wall and faced with the option of Christianity or death, generally accepted the Faith. Yet they refused to cooperate with the harsh occupation decrees of Frankish soldiers and churchmen. Charlemagne was forced to relax his stringent ordinances; thereafter the Saxons subsided, and Charlemagne's suzerainty was also recognized by many neighboring Slavic tribes living in what is now Poland.

Charlemagne's far-flung conquests doubled the size of the old Frankish kingdom and united under his personal rule a great diversity of peoples. His huge realm, together with its tributaries, very nearly coincided with what might be described as Christian Europe or Latin Christendom; by either description, its major lacks were only the Christian peoples of the British Isles and the Christian Spaniards ruled by the Muslims. Yet Charlemagne's contemporaries appear never to have thought of describing the extent of his dominion in terms of Latin Christendom—possibly because the sacrosanct indivisibility of Christendom kept them from making a distinction between the Church of Rome and the Eastern or Greek Church of Byzantium.

Available, however, was a convenient and self-explanatory term—empire; and Charlemagne received title to it in Rome on Christmas Day in the year 800. While the king was attending mass at St. Peter's basilica, Pope Leo III placed a crown on the monarch's head. The congregation chanted three times: "To Charles, the most pious Augustus, crowned by God, the great and peace-giving emperor, life and victory!" Then Leo prostrated himself before Charlemagne, a posture which until then had been a mark of reverence reserved for the theocratic emperor of Byzantium.

This ceremony, of brief duration and dubious legality, ranks among history's most significant events—and most intriguing puzzles. Apparently Charlemagne's contemporaries were at first confused about the significance of the coronation and the circumstances surrounding it; the blank spots and contradictions in their records leave many questions that may never be answered. Nevertheless, we have a good general idea of the tangled causes and effects of the ceremony.

The title of emperor, as Charlemagne and Pope Leo knew full well, belonged legally to the heir of the old Eastern Roman Empire, and only he could use or bestow it. Accepting that fact, Charlemagne had tried, through the 780s, to win Byzantine recognition of his status in the form of a dynastic marriage. His attempts had failed, but not nearly as badly as papal relations with Byzantium, which had been steadily worsening as the result of political and doctrinal disputes. By 795, when Leo became pope, he would have had little to lose and much to gain by usurping the imperial title and conferring it on his champion, Charlemagne. Even for Leo, however, the wish was not strong enough in 795 to justify the overt act.

But two years later, the parallel plans of king and pope were joined and precipitated by the sudden appearance of a legal loophole. In the strictly legal sense the throne of Byzantium became vacant in 797 when the Empress Irene usurped it from her son, Constantine VI. Because it was unprecedented for a mere woman to rule in her own name, many refused to recognize her as the legitimate successor. On this shaky basis, Charlemagne was probably willing to claim the title; in fact he might well have intended to crown himself without indebting himself to the pope for aid or sanction. But Leo shrewdly took the initiative. By crowning Charlemagne he not only invested the Frankish king with the fabled prestige of a Roman emperor, but at the same time he insinuated the thought that the very title of emperor was to be a gift of the papacy.

For Charlemagne, the coronation solved nothing. In 802, his legal loophole vanished when Irene was overthrown in favor of an unquestionably legal emperor. Until two years before Charlemagne's death in 814, he had to bargain doggedly before he was finally accepted as imperial "brother" by Emperor Michael of the new Byzantine dynasty.

The title of emperor made little real difference in the complexion of Charlemagne's reign. Of necessity, Charlemagne ruled in the same old Germanic way; that is, in the absence of any self-sustaining bureaucracy he governed as best he could through men bound to him by ties of personal loyalty. Indeed, Charlemagne, who was a great reformer rather than an innovator, made few additions to, or changes in, the institutions and policies he had inherited from Pepin and Charles Martel. Originality in government was not needed; improvement was, and this Charlemagne gave in

fuller measure than the West had known since the great days of Rome.

To increase the efficiency of his government Charlemagne tightened his hold on his officials and used them to keep each other honest. Within each administrative district, his government had two arms, secular and ecclesiastical; the counts and bishops alike swore loyalty to the king and were empowered, as independent and virtually equal colleagues, to initiate action on his behalf. In addition, Charlemagne periodically sent out to each district a two-man inspection team that reported directly to him on the accounts and performance of the local officials.

For the posts of count, bishop and inspector, Charlemagne sought the best men available; his only real precondition for royal service was personal loyalty. For all practical purposes, a man was not penalized—or preferred—for his social class or tribal ancestry. An outstanding Bavarian warrior might be appointed to serve as count beside a Frankish bishop in Lombard Italy; a humble Spanish cleric might wind up as an archbishop in the Frankish Church. This international interchange of personnel tended to homogenize administrative practices throughout the empire.

The tendency toward uniformity in government was reinforced by Charlemagne's handling of the law. He did not presume to abridge the ancient right of any of his peoples to live under their own legal code; but he did minimize the confusing diversity of tribal laws. This he accomplished by revising some of the codes and by ruling through a series of capitularies, or decrees, which were enforced under all codes.

Charlemagne's reforms also extended into the field of economics. To discourage profiteering and speculation in commodities, he prohibited transactions made at night and fixed maximum prices for grains in bulk. He even went so far as to fix the price that bakers could charge for their bread. To facilitate trade on the local level, Charlemagne issued coins of a standard denomination and metal content; these largely replaced the diverse and debased coinage previously used in the lands comprising his empire.

During Charlemagne's reign, long-distance trade staged a modest upturn despite the disruptive effects of Muslim control of Mediterranean shipping lanes. Indeed it was because the Mediterranean was a Muslim sea that Charles gave legal protection to the Jewish merchants, who, being identified with neither Islam nor Christendom, served as invaluable middlemen between the hostile worlds. In the long run, Charles' guarantees to the Jewish traders helped to make business respectable and to foster the development of the new merchant class whose commerce was to galvanize Europe in the 11th Century. But in Charlemagne's day, long-distance trade remained a minor traffic specializing in such luxury items as Eastern spices and silks.

The economy of early medieval Europe was heavily agrarian, and it was in agriculture that it made its greatest gains in Carolingian times. The labor of man and animal began increasing in efficiency through the use of such rediscovered inventions as the water mill and the heavy plow enabling deeper cultivation. The introduction of the three-field system, which allowed each of three subdivisions of an arable tract to lay fallow in successive seasons, slowly raised the yield per acre. As the forests were pushed back, the scale of farming rose on the great estates of the Church and the nobility, and also in the clusters of small freeholdings centered on villages.

There is no better example of the growing agrarian efficiency of the Eighth Century than Charlemagne's own estates—and by one accounting he owned 1,615 of them. Under the king's scrutiny, capable stewards managed the royal estates so well

that Charlemagne's profits from them, together with his war booty and rich gifts from his supporters, permitted him to run his government without imposing a general money tax on his subjects whose dues to the throne were paid in service. Indeed the only tax in the usual sense that he required was the sacramental tithe that landowners paid to the Church in produce.

By modern Western standards Charlemagne's Europe was neither prosperous nor especially productive; yet some contemporaries had ample reason for thinking it was both. Considerable numbers of peasants benefited from the opening and organized colonization of eastern lands conquered by Charlemagne's armies. Plague and famine still killed thousands as they had always done; but Europe's population would sink no lower. With good Christian wars to be fought on the frontiers, with peace and order enforced at home, most of the landed and the literate minorities could not deny that "Europe" had taken a turn for the better, and that they owed their well-being largely to their just and powerful protector, Charlemagne.

Charlemagne himself was not deluded by the traces of affluence and solidity that dignified his realm. Secure prosperity, he had realized early in his reign, depended on the development of literate and responsible government officials. As the need for such men increased apace with his conquests, he put all of his resources and prestige behind a campaign to prepare the sons of noblemen for high administrative posts, secular and ecclesiastical. These efforts, prompted by necessity, far outreached their limited goal and gave impetus to a cultural revival whose effects long outlasted his empire. This was the so-called "Carolingian renaissance."

The problems of increasing the supply of literate men in an era marked by its paucity of education might have discouraged a less-determined king. When Charlemagne came to the throne secular edu-

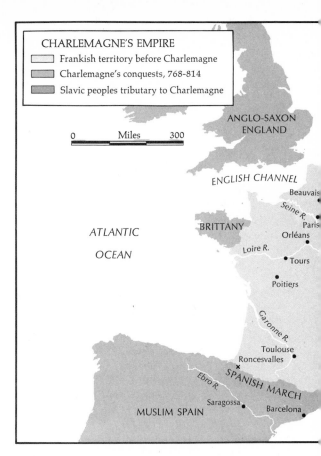

THE FRANKISH REALM *was already the strongest barbarian state when Charlemagne became king in 768. In 60 campaigns he expanded it to the north, east and south, and many Slavic peoples*

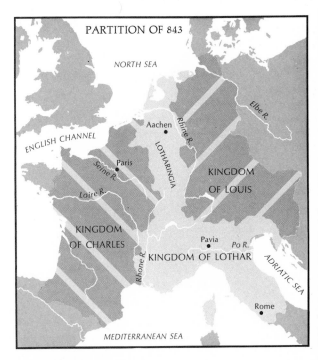

FRAGMENTATION *wrecked the empire that Charlemagne left to his son Louis. In 843, after Louis' death, the realm was divided among Louis' sons: Charles the Bald, Lothar and Louis the German.*

cation had practically disappeared throughout the West. Even in the Church, the percentage of literate clerics and the average level of their education had declined nearly everywhere. Ireland was an exception and so was England, where Irish and Italian missionaries had successfully transplanted the seeds of learning in the early Seventh Century. Nowhere, however, had the number of literate men declined more sharply than in the Frankish kingdom. Charlemagne had to revive education in his realm before he could educate officials.

Contributing to the dismal state of education at the outset of Charlemagne's reign was the turmoil of the post-Roman times. Through wars, raids and plain neglect, teachers and scholars had been robbed of vital tools of their trade; many a manuscript had been ruined, and a number of Classical treasures—including substantial portions of the works of Livy and Virgil—had been lost forever.

Another obstacle to education in the Eighth Century was the mechanical difficulties of learning and teaching. Language alone was a terrible problem, for political fragmentation and regional isolation had produced a near Babel of tongues. Charlemagne, himself, having been raised in the un-Romanized Rhineland, spoke as his native tongue the Germanic dialect of the Eastern Franks, but he had to know what amounted to a second language in order to understand the Western Franks, who spoke late Latin dialects. Moreover, these Latin vernaculars were in rapid transition, developing into early forms of the Romance (from "Roman") languages—French, Italian, Provençal, Spanish and Portuguese. The Classical Latin of Roman literature was fast becoming a dead language that had to be learned in a classroom much as it is today.

To carry out his revival of education, Charlemagne offered handsome rewards and unlimited support to eminent scholars and teachers within his own empire and in neighboring lands, and

beyond its eastern border acknowledged his overlordship. Recognizing Charlemagne's rule over most of what had been Roman Europe, Pope Leo III crowned him Emperor of the Romans in 800.

PARTITION in 888 further divided the Frankish realm into five kingdoms, after a reunification in 885. Arbitrary divisions into petty states would plague Western Europe into modern times.

gradually he assembled a devoted international cadre. From Italy came the grammarian Peter of Pisa, the historian Paul the Deacon and a group of Roman music teachers whose particular assignment was to refine the singing of Frankish church choirs. The Visigothic poet Theodulf came north from the Spanish border and served imaginatively as bishop of Orléans. Eginhard, an Eastern Frank noted both for his diminutive size and for his historical works, came to round out his studies and stayed on as one of Charlemagne's advisors and later served him as minister of public works. Ireland was represented by contingents of zealous scholars. But it was England, the country that had become the first in scholarship by the later Eighth Century, which gave Charlemagne's revival its cultural captain—the Anglo-Saxon Alcuin of York.

In Alcuin, Charlemagne found a sort of clerical replica of himself. Formerly director of studies at what was then the West's foremost center of learning—the cathedral school at York—Alcuin was at once a superb organizer, an inspiring leader, a versatile and tireless worker. Serving at court from about 782 to 796 with two respites, Alcuin was the king's chief advisor on diplomatic and religious affairs, co-author and director of the royal educational program, and coordinator and arbiter of cultural activities throughout the Frankish domains.

Alcuin's first step was to prime the fountainhead of the Carolingian revival, the so-called palace school at Charlemagne's capital of Aachen (Aix-la-Chapelle). This institution dated back to the time of Charles Martel (714-741) or perhaps earlier, but its curriculum had never included much beyond the arts of war. Under Alcuin it became a school for aspirants to high office and for career scholars and teachers. Adolescent sons of noblemen, and a few of their mustachioed fathers, attended classes that were probably seminarlike and studied what was henceforth to be the basic medieval curriculum

FROM ORNAMENTATION TO STIRRING IMAGES:
THE CHANGING MEDIEVAL MANUSCRIPT

DECORATIVE ILLUSTRATIONS *for religious texts were fashioned in the Eighth Century by Irish monks, who glorified the word of God with rich, stylized designs. At right are pages from the Book of Kells, done about 800. On one, the four Evangelists are represented by symbols. The other page is lettered in a script so ornate that it is difficult to read.*

REALISTIC REPRESENTATION *reappeared in Europe during Charlemagne's reign. Turning toward Byzantine and Roman precedents, artists began to depict the Evangelists as human beings, as in the portrayals of St. Mark and St. John flanking the central illustrations at right. The picture at top center shows a script that is more readable; below it is seen a small but clear painting of the Ascension of Christ, framed in an easily distinguished capital "C."*

NARRATIVE PICTURES, *painted in realistic style, became common in Charlemagne's time. At right is a Ninth Century sequence telling the story of the Fall of Adam and Eve. At far right an 11th Century illumination shows a later style that flourished in northern Europe. In depicting an angel announcing the Nativity, the artist created a vivid, moving portrayal of a Biblical event.*

—the seven "liberal" arts of Classical antiquity.

The course was divided into two groups of subjects: the *quadrivium*—arithmetic, geometry, astronomy and music; and the *trivium*—rhetoric, grammar and logic. In practice, the course was less comprehensive than it sounds. The *quadrivium* was taught only perfunctorily because the cardinal Greek works on science were largely unavailable in Latin translation, and the study of Greek had lapsed almost entirely. The *trivium* amounted to little more than a study of Latin and its usage through Roman literature. Yet even this meager fare was a feast for an aristocracy with a long record of intellectual starvation. The young lords needed little encouragement from Alcuin and his staff to plunge into lively discussion; and Charlemagne, who enjoyed attending class between military campaigns and administrative tours, often joined in with sallies of his own, and with praise or reproof for the discourse of others.

The enthusiasm and camaraderie of the palace school spilled over into the court itself. Members of the official family called Aachen the "second Rome" and the "second Athens," and they addressed and referred to each other by Classical or Biblical names. Alcuin was "Horace" and Charlemagne was dubbed "David," after the psalm-singing Old Testament king. The hours of informal socializing at court often presented the incongruous spectacle of war-hardened lords, pious clerics and notorious womanizers (none more so than Charlemagne himself) engaging in self-improvement, testing each other with riddles, bright repartee and scraps of ancient pagan poetry.

Education was far more than a fad of the court. It was Charlemagne's will and therefore the empire's command, and gradually it spread beyond Aachen to regional centers. In the see of Orléans, for example, Bishop Theodulf instructed the priests of certain villages and estates to hold classes that the local populace could attend without charge. Although the results are little known and presumably meager, Theodulf certainly ranks as one of the earliest exponents of free public education. Other high churchmen, inspired by the palace school or intimidated by its royal backer, wrote to Alcuin requesting information on how to upgrade instruction in their monastic or cathedral schools. In answer, Alcuin kept up a steady flow of letters offering encouragement and homely tips on the content and art of proper pedagogy. He recommended, among other things, that classes be kept small and closely supervised "lest the boys, enjoying leisure, stray unattended all over the place, play foolish games, or are free to indulge in other silly tricks."

The palace school at Aachen, and others modeled after it, did the limited job that Charlemagne demanded—with something to spare. They provided more and better officials for church and state, and they produced most of the best teachers and scholars of the next generation. However, the creative endeavors of Charlemagne's scholars clearly show the narrow horizons of the Carolingian revival. Alcuin and his colleagues and pupils had too much to learn from the past to contribute much of originality to the future.

In writing and scholarship, the Carolingians were at best talented imitators, skilled collators and imaginative interpreters. They composed poetry in the Classical Roman modes, and while most of it was mediocre, some informal verses by Bishop Theodulf of Orléans display a wry, worldly wit unique for the time. One of their few studies in the sciences, an encyclopedic work by Hrabanus Maurus, an outstanding pupil of Alcuin, is interesting chiefly because it proves that a handful of early medieval Europeans had not yet forgotten one key fact known to the ancients: the world is round. The palace scholars did produce a major work of biography, Eginhard's life of Charlemagne; and it was heavily salted with phrases adapted from Suetonius' life of the Roman Emperor Augustus. The greater energies of most scholars, however, were devoted to studies of the scriptures and the books of the Church Fathers. These were perused and interpreted endlessly, and the consequence was a vast output of sermons, didactic essays, theological dissertations and allegorical tracts.

If Charlemagne's savants contributed little to scholarship that was altogether original, to them must go credit for completing a much-needed overhaul in medieval handwriting style. The earliest medieval manuscripts had been written on Egyptian papyrus and in large Roman letters. But when Muslim control of the Mediterranean interrupted the papyrus supply, Europeans were obliged to write on far more costly parchment; and to economize on space, scholars condensed the large Roman characters into small, compact ones. Several regions, notably Ireland and Anglo-Saxon England, developed fine minuscule or small-letter writing systems of their own, but that of the Franks was singularly illegible and unattractive. Around 750, efforts were made to improve it, and the task of consolidating and promoting these reforms fell to Alcuin and his associates.

Under their direction, monks perfected the so-called Carolingian minuscule—a script that was compact yet graceful and above all legible and easy to write. With Charlemagne's endorsement, the new minuscule possessed the means for international dissemination, and within two decades it had replaced all others in writing centers throughout the Frankish empire. Before the turn of the 12th Century, it had even triumphed in Ireland and in England.

Enormous credit must also be given the scholars of Charlemagne's time for rediscovering and preserving many works of antiquity that might otherwise have been lost to the world. Encouraged by the king, the abbots of Carolingian monasteries ferreted out rare Roman works. These Classical treasures were concealed in the hassocks and baggage of intrepid monks and carried on dangerous journeys to distant monasteries for study and copying. The actual work of transcription was literally endless. Even using the new compact and legible minuscule style of handwriting, one trained scribe might take three or four months to copy a single work of average length. In some scriptoria, twelve or more copyists were kept busy all year round. But by dint of their painstaking toil, at least a dozen monasteries had accumulated "large" libraries of a few hundred volumes by the end of the Ninth Century. The size and distribution of these libraries guaranteed the hard-won rediscoveries of Carolingian scholars. No Roman work that had survived long enough to be copied by Charlemagne's scholars was subsequently lost. It is to these volumes, transcribed in the graceful minuscule style, that we owe our entire heritage of the writings of Caesar, Tacitus, Juvenal, Martial and many other Classical authors.

As the copies of ancient works increased in quantity they also improved in quality. When possible, scholars obtained and compared two manuscripts of the same work, thus freeing the copied version from many errors that had crept into the text. Moreover, many of the scribes' copies were transformed into works of art by other specialists. The initial letters were colored by rubricators and decorated by illuminators, and the most talented illuminators enriched margins and full pages with their dazzling inventions.

The illumination of manuscripts—and all Carolingian art—was highly eclectic. Sometimes motifs and artistic styles from several sources can be detected on a single page—perhaps an ornate Anglo-Saxon border, an intricate tracery borrowed from Irish art, even a geometric design that found its way out of the Scandinavian north. But by far the most dramatic feature of Carolingian illuminations was the renewed importance given to the portrayal of the human figure after centuries of eclipse in the West under the Germanic barbarians, who generally preferred abstract and animal motifs and seldom showed the faces and figures of men. In this vital step toward humanism in art, painters depicted the saints with the realistic detail that had characterized Roman portraiture or with the stylized flatness of Byzantine art. A further step was taken by Carolingian artisans who created Biblical scenes in low-relief on boxes, book covers, vessels and other objects of ivory or gold. Only after another five centuries or so of medieval progress would the human form be generally carved in the round, as a free-standing statue.

As the creations of the Carolingian artists and craftsmen helped to establish new principles in Western art, so did the architecture of Charlemagne's day lead to new and unifying themes in church construction. This is not readily apparent, for at first glance the religious buildings of the Carolingians seem even more diverse and derivative than their manuscript art. The most celebrated example—the domed octagonal chapel that Charlemagne built for his palace at Aachen—was modeled after a Byzantine church and in its upper portions used Roman columns to support tiers of arches. And Germigny des Prés, the squat little church that Bishop Theodulf built outside Orléans, includes not only a Byzantine mosaic but also "Moorish" horseshoe arches—a development of the Visigoths and not, as popularly believed, a feature brought to Spain by the Muslim conquerors.

In spite of their varied stylistic ingredients, however, the churches of the period shared fundamental features that stamp Carolingian architecture as a new and original synthesis—the first truly European architecture. For while most Carolingian churches imitated Roman architecture, their unifying innovations reflected the new religious spirit that was sweeping the West—the veneration of the saints.

These innovations were an outgrowth of the great medieval pilgrimages. By Charlemagne's time, ever increasing numbers of the faithful were traveling far and wide to pray at the special shrines of their favorite saints. The journeys of worshipers—especially to Rome, to the tomb of St. James the Apostle at Santiago de Compostella in northwestern Spain and points along the routes to both places—put mounting pressure on the great pilgrimage churches—and on the Carolingian builders. The fundamental floor plan of each church was that of the rectangular Roman basilica and usually included an apse (that rounded portion of the church behind the main altar) and a transept (the lateral extensions that give a church its symbolic cruciform shape). To accommodate the pilgrims, the builders added little chapels dedicated to the saints, eventually extending these from the apse so that in plan it showed a scalloped outline. A semicircular passageway, or ambulatory, curving around the apse gave access to the chapels, and was connected to arcaded aisles along either side of the nave—the main body of the church. Thus the pilgrims could enter the church from the front and go about their private devotions without interfering with ceremonies in progress in the nave. The ambulatory and the apse with radiating chapels became increasingly important parts of Carolingian architecture and they spread throughout the West.

Whenever Charlemagne ordered the construction of a church, whether in Saxon Germany or Lombard Italy, the plans cleared his royal workshop and therefore conformed to a canon of style set by Alcuin, Eginhard and other tastemakers. Some new churches in the Carolingian style were also built unofficially in northern Spain and even in Rome. Each region, however, perpetuated its own local peculiarities of construction and decoration, and would continue to do so after the Carolingian innovations were absorbed into the Romanesque architecture of the 11th Century. In parts of northern France, for instance, the local Frankish masons preferred to build church walls of patterned brickwork. In Germany, Carolingian builders favored churches with lofty, tower-flanked fronts—a taste that prevailed there even in Gothic architecture after the 12th Century. Yet these massive structures, no less than the palace church at Aachen, are unmistakably Carolingian, and they communicate the same mood of stolid masculinity and crude grandeur.

Charlemagne's chapel at Aachen served as the setting for the final act of the great king's reign. There, on January 28, 814, his ponderous corpse was buried, reportedly sitting bolt upright on a throne. Charlemagne's death was not untimely: he was about 72, and accounts of his last years convey the impression that he was none too sorry to leave this world. A terrible famine that swept his empire in 809, the death of his sons Pepin in 810 and Charles in 811, his long-drawn-out bargaining with the Byzantines to legalize the title of emperor for his sole surviving son Louis— these seem to have overtaxed Charlemagne's stamina and resolve. Some historians conclude that the king had grown senile. A less likely explanation, suggested by a chronicler of the later Ninth Century, is that Charlemagne succumbed to premonitions of disaster at the sight of Viking ships, which raided his shores with increasing boldness in the last decade of his reign.

In quite another context, the Vikings and other marauders did demonstrate forcefully the limitations of Charlemagne's strength and the integral weaknesses of his empire. When he crushed the nautical Frisians, Charlemagne threw the North Sea wide open to the Vikings. Similarly, his crushing of the Avars in Central Europe helped pave the way

west for the Magyars, new invaders from beyond the Urals, and his absorption of the Saxons exposed his northeastern frontier to resurgent Slavs. What is more, his far-flung conquests consumed so much treasure, manpower and travel time that he never got around to subduing completely the Celts of the Brittany peninsula, right in his own backyard.

Charlemagne's empire was, in fact, a giant dying of its own great size—and of his very efforts to preserve it. As Charlemagne increased the efficiency of his government, he also increased the capability of its local officials to resist his successors. Even the Carolingian revival worked against the empire. While it helped to unite many peoples of Europe with a common Latin and Christian culture, it also deepened their awareness of the ethnic self-interests and cultural differences that divided them.

In one sense, then, Charlemagne's Europe may be called a false start or a grandiose failure. Its cultural heritage survived to inspire future generations. But politically it was bound to crumble and then be rebuilt into a totally different structure. From the myriad of fragments would arise not an empire, but a collection of nation-states.

Still, the great concepts of Charlemagne's age lived on, strengthened by his reign. In various parts of his former dominions, the imperial idea would persist as a political force until 1806, when, under the name of the Holy Roman Empire, it was terminated by another self-styled emperor, Napoleon I. The idea of Christendom also gained substance and definition from the fact that Charlemagne's unitary rule had extended over most of the Christian West. Indeed the growth of Christendom eclipsed the term "Europe" for centuries, but the connection between Charlemagne and "Europe" survived. In 1095 Pope Urban II preached the First Crusade to free the Holy Land from the "infidels." He called upon all Christian warriors of Europe to do their duty as worthy sons of "Charles surnamed the great."

"THE SONG OF ROLAND"

In 778, Charlemagne crossed the Pyrenees and subdued several Muslim-held cities in northern Spain. While returning to France, the rear guard of his army was ambushed by Basque freebooters in the mountain pass of Roncesvalles; among the dead was Roland, Prefect of Brittany. Over the next few hundred years this minor action grew into a heroic legend that inspired two of feudal Europe's greatest works of art: *The Song of Roland*, a rousing 11th Century epic poem, and the stained-glass "Charlemagne Window" in the Cathedral of Chartres. Both works —combined on these pages in fragments from the originals—transformed Charles' simple military campaign into a holy Crusade, and the Muslims into Roland's murderers. Above, the king is flanked by Roland and Archbishop Turpin of Rheims, as they set out on their fabled war against the hated "Paynim" (pagan).

Photographs by Pierre Belzeaux.

"Paynims and Franks
—behold them joined in war"

"Charles the great King, lord of the land of France,
Has fought beyond the hills for seven years,
And led his conquering host to the land's end.
There is but one of all the towns of Spain
Unshattered—grim Saragossa, mountain-girt,
Held by Marsila, King of Spain, of those
Who love not God and serve false gods of stone
Brought from the shores of Araby.—Hapless King!
Your hour is come, for all your gods of stone! . . .
"And [Charles] spake, and said: 'Fair sirs, to us
The Paynim sends his messengers, with store
Of precious gifts, lions and shaggy bears,
Camels and falcons, mules weighed down with gold
Of Araby—more than we may take away
In fifty of our wains. But he demands
We turn again to our own land, and he
Will follow us straightway, and there subscribe
In all things to our law and glorious faith,
Turn Christian, be my liegeman—ay, and yet
I fathom not his real intent.' He spake,
And the Franks cried: 'It is a trap—take heed!' "

WHILE IN SPAIN, THE "SONG" RELATES, THE FRANKS FOUGHT MANY BATTLES;
IN THIS DETAIL FROM THE CHARLEMAGNE WINDOW, ROLAND (LEFT, IN RED
COAT) IMPALES AN ENEMY KNIGHT, WHO SLUMPS OVER HIS HORSE. AT LAST
THE FRANKS MASSED BEFORE SARAGOSSA, THE STRONGHOLD OF KING MAR-
SILA. EAGER FOR PEACE, THE KING SENT EMISSARIES TO CHARLES WITH
PRECIOUS GIFTS AND PROMISES OF SUBMISSION IF HE WOULD LEAVE SPAIN.

"The host of Charles the King was marching home"

"So the night passed, and day dawned bright again;
  And through the marshalled ranks of his great host
  [Charles] rode, and cried: 'Soldiers, against the sun
  Rises the blessed pass of Roncesvalles,
  Winding across the hills to France. And whom
  Shall we elect, my lords, to guard the rear?'
  Then quickly Ganelon spake: 'Let Roland stay . . .
"And the King wept, and all his men were filled
  With a great fear for Roland, lest his life
  Be meanly sold for silver and for gold
  By Ganelon, and garments of fair silk,
  And horses, and strange beasts from overseas.—
  And now the Paynim King, with hope renewed,
  Had gathered fighting-men from every town
  And furthest part of Spain, a fearful horde.
  To Saragossa's highest battlement
  They hoisted a stone god, and prayed. Then rode,
  Each vying with the other, over hill
  And through deep valleys, till they came at last
  To Roncesvalles . . ."

WARILY ACCEPTING MARSILA'S OFFER, CHARLES SENT COUNT GANELON TO
NEGOTIATE. BUT GANELON TOLD MARSILA THAT CHARLES WOULD TIRE OF
WAR ONLY IF ROLAND, HIS FAVORITE (AND GANELON'S HATED RIVAL), WAS
KILLED. TOGETHER THEY PLOTTED ROLAND'S DEATH AT THE HEAD OF THE
REAR GUARD. CHARLES, UNAWARE OF THE TREACHERY AND RECEIVING AS-
SURANCES OF MARSILA'S VASSALAGE, TURNED BACK FOR FRANCE (RIGHT).

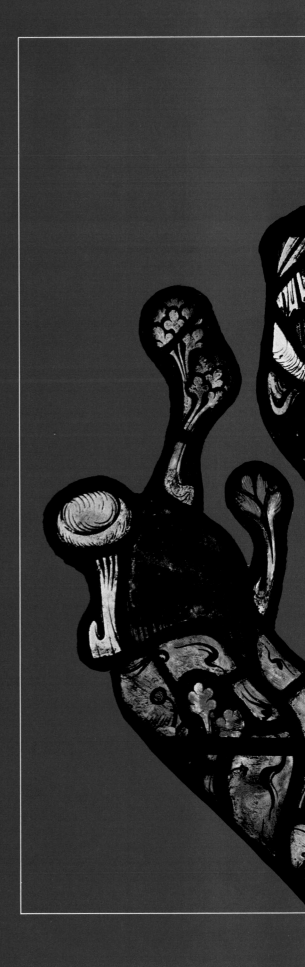

"Lay on, soldiers of France!
This day we win or die!"

"The day was clear, resplendent shone the sun,
Each several bit of armor flamed again.
And all the trumpets of the host rang loud;
The echoing rumor, borne on the west wind,
Found out the straight defile of Roncesvalles . . .
"The battle raged full wild and wondrously.
In wrath the Franks fought on. They thrust and hewed,
And found, beneath the glittering coats of mail,
The flesh and bone. And the red blood ran down . . .
Four battles did they fight, and win—the fifth
Went not so well. Alas, of all the Franks
Sixty alone are left, whom God has spared
Till now—and dearly will they sell their lives. . . .
"And Roland, with a wild and fearful blast
Winded his horn, so that his temples brake
And from his mouth leapt the bright blood. And Charles
Heard it, and all his soldiers, as they rode
Down to sweet France through valleys far away.
And the King cried: 'It is the horn of Roland!
The Franks are fighting. . . .'"

AS THE FRANKISH REAR GUARD FILED THROUGH THE NARROW PASS, THEY
WERE ATTACKED BY WAVES OF MUSLIM WARRIORS, 400,000 STRONG, AC-
CORDING TO THE LEGEND. ROLAND AND HIS SMALL BAND OF KNIGHTS VAL-
IANTLY ENGAGED THE ENEMY IN SINGLE COMBAT (RIGHT), BUT THE ODDS
WERE TOO GREAT. WHEN ONLY A FEW FRANKS WERE LEFT ALIVE, ROLAND,
AT LAST, SOUNDED HIS HORN SO THAT CHARLES WOULD KNOW HIS PLIGHT.

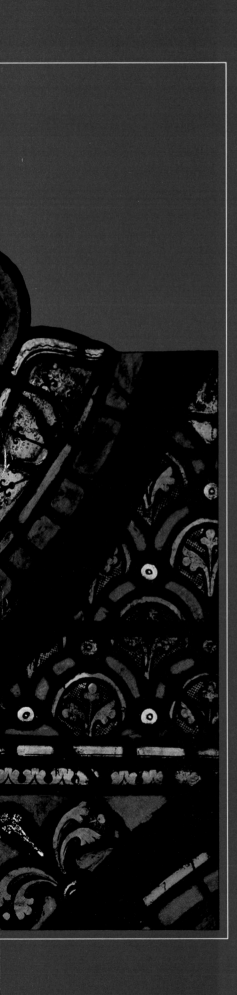

"From his wounds
a crimson flood was flowing"

"The Paynims cried: 'The King is coming. Hark!
The Frankish clarions near at hand are ringing.
If the King comes in time, and Roland lives,
This fearful war will start anew, and we
Shall lose forever the fair land of Spain.'
Four hundred banded them together, ay,
Four hundred of the best, and all at once
On Roland charged—four hundred against one. . . .
"And likewise Roland dealt good blows. But now
Fever consumed his strength and in his head
Was fearful torment . . .
"And then he knew that death was taking hold
Of his great frame, creeping from head to heart. . . .
Under a lofty pine he lay, and turned
Toward Spain, and called to memory many things—
The lands that he had conquered, and sweet France,
His kindred, and Great Charles, who cherished him
As his own son. . . ."

AT THE SOUND OF THE HORN, CHARLES, FEARING FOR ROLAND'S LIFE, RE-
TURNED TO HELP WHILE THE "PAYNIMS" REDOUBLED THEIR EFFORTS, SEND-
ING A LAST MASSIVE CHARGE AGAINST HIM. ONE BY ONE THE FRANKISH
KNIGHTS FELL UNTIL ROLAND WAS LEFT ALMOST ALONE. SORELY WOUND-
ED, THE HALOED HERO RESTS UPON HIS SHIELD (LEFT), CLUTCHING HIS
SWORD, DURENDAL, AS HE IS ATTENDED BY ANOTHER SAINTLY KNIGHT.

"And so the angels came on wings of gold to take his soul to God"

"And Roland, though his eyes were dimmed, though death
Was near at hand, gathered strength once more,
And stood upon his feet. Before him lay
A marble stone. In pain and fearful wrath
He swung bright Durendal, and smote upon
The unyielding rock. The quivering steel rang loud,
But broke not . . . He raised his horn once more,
And feebly winded it. And the King heard,
And reined his steed, and said: 'Hearken, my lords.
It fares not well with Roland—he is dying.
He would not wind so feebly, had he long
To live. If you would reach the field, give spur
To your good steeds. And let the clarions sound . . .'
"Roland is dead. In heaven his great soul rests
With God his Father. And now the King had come
To Roncesvalles, and found nor road nor path,
Nor bit of field an ell or foot in width,
Where lay not stretched in death a Saracen
Or Frank. And the King called in a loud voice:
'Where are you, Roland?' . . . But what availed his words?
For none could answer them. . . ."

IN A FINAL DESPERATE EFFORT, ROLAND ROSE FROM A BATTLEFIELD STREWN
WITH THE ENEMIES HE HAD SLAIN. VAINLY HE TRIED TO DESTROY HIS HAL-
LOWED SWORD ON A ROCK (AT LEFT), THEN SOUNDED HIS HORN FOR THE
LAST TIME (RIGHT). CHARLES ARRIVED, TOO LATE, BUT PURSUED MARSILA'S
ARMY AND DEFEATED IT. LATER, IN FRANCE, THE "SONG" CONCLUDES, THE
TRAITOROUS GANELON WAS TRIED IN COURT—AND TORN LIMB FROM LIMB.

6

THE VIKING MARAUDERS

Two generations after the death of Charlemagne, churches throughout Western Europe were echoing to a new prayer, "From the wrath of the Northmen, O Lord, deliver us!" For this was the great age of the barbarian Vikings who descended upon the continent in a wild orgy of plunder and mayhem.

Emerging from the bleak Scandinavian north, the original homeland of the earlier Germanic tribesmen who had assaulted Rome, the Vikings too found a crumbling empire. In this case it was the Frankish state, and the Vikings' unpredictable seaborne attacks speeded up its disintegration. Once again churchmen saw in the barbarian depredations the demise of Western civilization, and they construed the Viking menace as a divine punishment for society's sins. And once again the marauders, who came first as destroyers and later as invaders, stayed to become colonists. By the mid-10th Century, Danes, Swedes and Norwegians were helping to revitalize Europe's commerce with their genius for trade, and some of their descendants, the Normans, would play a leading role in bringing new order to Western Europe's shattered political structure.

Despite fervent prayers for divine deliverance, nothing stayed the Vikings or altered their course. Under reckless and heroic leaders with ominous names—Eric Bloodax, Harald Bluetooth, Ivar the Boneless—they ravaged far and wide. The range and impact of their onslaughts are suggested by the violent visits they paid to towns of Western Europe. Among the dozens of communities that fell to the raiders were towns as far apart as London, Cádiz and Pisa. Viking forces overwhelmed Bordeaux and Paris, captured Rheims and Rouen, sacked and burned Aachen and Cologne. Between 853 and 903 they put Tours to the sword six times.

What propelled the Scandinavians onto the stage of history with such sudden and destructive force? The causes are as obscure as the derivation of the name "Viking" itself (signifying one who goes adventuring by sea, in medieval Scandinavian languages). Most scholars agree that one important factor was overpopulation. In the Second Century, when many Germanic tribes—ethnic and linguistic cousins of the Northmen—began their migrations southward, they left Scandinavia thinly peopled. For a long time thereafter it remained a virtual wilderness, scattered with crude villages that subsisted mainly on farming, supplemented by fishing and a little trade. But the population rose slowly and formed new settlements. Since Scandinavia's inland regions are mountainous and inhospitable, these were largely limited to the narrow coastal bands. As the population continued to grow, the settlements were bound to overflow.

Undoubtedly overpopulation was not the sole cause of the Viking phenomenon. As the Northmen's trade increased, they must have been animated by a growing taste for wealth as well as by their inherent and irresistible urge to go adventuring. Apparently, too, a combination of customs added a volatile element to the expanding pool of surplus manpower. Many Scandinavian chieftains practiced polygamy and adhered to a rule of inheritance by primogeniture. Their numerous younger sons, disinherited, made up a large and dangerous warrior elite who were obliged to make their own way by any means, be it conquests at home or piracy abroad. Presumably this group supplied most of the leaders for the Vikings' descent upon Europe.

Whatever the cause, the Eighth Century brought steadily mounting pressures within Scandinavia. These produced a marked increase not only in trading activity through the northern seas, in obscure wars for land and power between the northern kings and their chieftains, but also in piratical raids. What may be the earliest account of a recognizable Viking raid comes from a contemporary Anglo-Saxon chronicle which reports that in 789 there came to England the "first three ships of the Northmen from the land of robbers."

The Eighth Century also ensured the future triumphs of the Northmen by bringing to perfection the design of their vessels. What had begun as an oar-driven, round-bottomed boat became the versatile Viking "longship," complete with sail and keel.

The sleek new craft must be counted among the finest technological developments of the Early Middle Ages. From a number of unearthed ships, including specimens buried intact as funerary chambers, it is known that by around 900 the typical Viking war-galley was a deckless, 30-oared affair, averaging about 70 feet in length and 16 feet at the beam. Such a craft could make 10 knots under its one big sail; it could accommodate nearly 100 men and yet be handled on the open sea by as few as 15. It was nimble enough to skirt shore defenses, capacious enough for lucrative plundering expeditions, sturdy enough to make stormy Atlantic crossings. Its shallow draft enabled it to navigate far inland on the rivers of Europe, and it was light enough to be dragged overland past fortified bridges.

To the Scandinavians, the Viking ship was even more than the perfect vehicle for warfare as well as trade. It was a revered possession upon which they often lavished the best of their vigorous art, carving awesome figureheads of dragons or wild animals and adding wooden or metal trim exquisitely worked with sophisticated abstract designs. Their preliterate bards apostrophized the ship and handed down by word of mouth a vivid poetry glorifying the act of sailing it and those who dared to challenge the sea. Nowhere is the Viking's exultation in his ship more graphically expressed than in the great epic of the Scandinavian hero Beowulf:

He gave command for a goodly vessel
Fitted and furnished . . .
Came the hour of boarding; the boat was riding
The waves of the harbor under the hill.
The eager mariners mounted the prow;
Billows were breaking, sea against sand.
In the ship's hold snugly they stowed their trappings,
Gleaming armor and battle-gear;
Launched the vessel, the well-braced bark,
Seaward bound on a joyous journey.
Over breaking billows, with bellying sail
And foamy beak, like a flying bird
The ship sped on. . . .

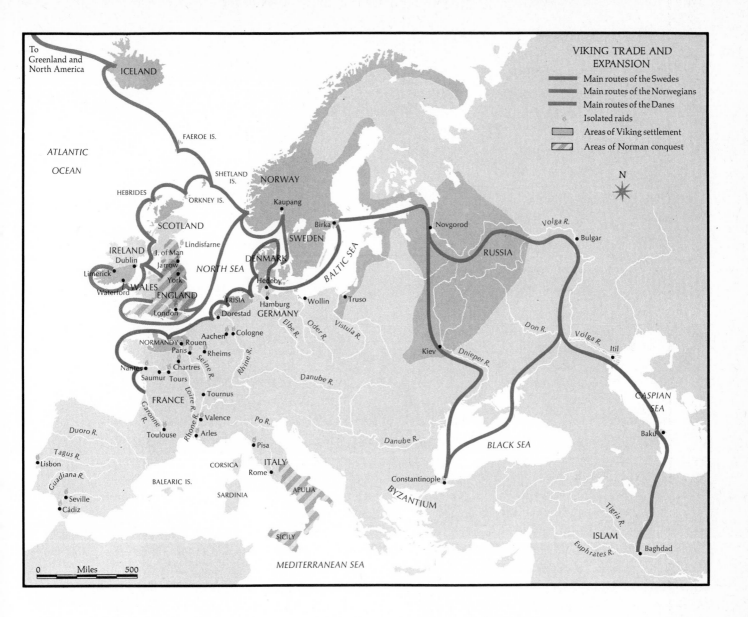

Indeed, the special kind of freedom that these marvelous ships gave the Scandinavians helped to shape their character almost as much as the northland's long nights, harsh winters and bleak terrain.

For better and for worse, the Scandinavians were fervent individualists. Their tribal societies recognized kings, noblemen, freemen and slaves, yet the Northmen stoutly and illogically maintained, "We are all equal." All too often, they proved their independence and their disdain for authority by drowning a king or removing him by some other equally violent means. The essence of their spirit is well summed up in a saga in which a Viking warrior describes his religion. He might have said that he worships warlike gods and nature-spirits;

this was the fact of the matter. Instead he voices a greater truth: "I believe in my own strength."

The Scandinavians were also the archetypal barbarians. Not only did the Vikings condone polygamy and worship such heathen deities as Odin, god of war and wisdom, and the storm-god Thor, they often cremated their dead and occasionally practiced human sacrifice. Sometimes a man's wife was slain to accompany him in death or a wealthy man's funeral pyre might include a slave girl.

In battle the Scandinavians displayed a terrifying ferocity that made them blind to danger and at times to leadership. During the earlier Viking raids they fought with very little teamwork; our word "berserk" stems from *berserkr*, the name of a class

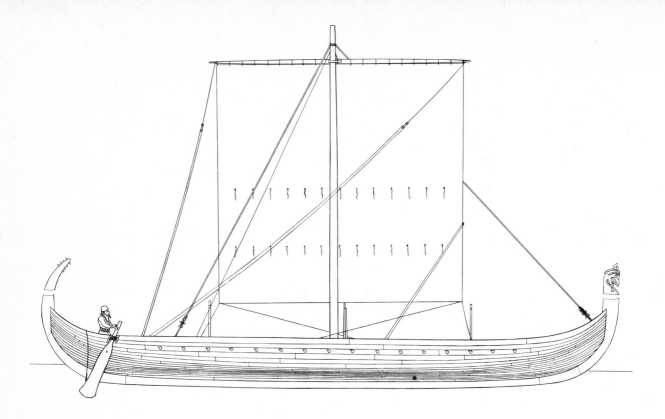

of warrior-fanatics who often wore bearshirts and who charged into battle in a frenzy that made them oblivious to their own wounds—and to their leaders' commands. The Vikings set no premium on indiscriminate killing, but they had a fine contempt for an indication of mercy. One warrior, for example, won from his fellows the scornful nickname, "the children's man," because he declined to partake in their practice of tossing the babies of conquered enemies into the air and catching them on the point of a spear. Many tales of Viking atrocities were no doubt exaggerated by their victims, but it seems clear that the Northmen had fewer scruples than their Germanic precursors.

Around 800, the dawn of the Viking Age, the Swedes, Norwegians and Danes embarked on separate courses that were largely predetermined by the special talents of each people and by the lay of their land. The Swedes, gifted traders whose settlements faced east on the Baltic, pushed into northern Russia and sailed south along the Volga and Dnieper. At Novgorod, Kiev and other towns they established trading posts and stocked them with such Scandinavian goods as otter, marten and beaver pelts, amber and walrus ivory, as well as slaves, honey and furs obtained from the Slavic natives

for hundreds of miles around. From their Russian bases, Swedish Vikings carried their wares to Constantinople and even to Baghdad and other cities of the Muslim East. The exotic goods they brought back to Scandinavia attracted merchants from many parts of Western Europe. To such bustling market centers as Birka in eastern Sweden came German, Frisian and Frankish traders and Anglo-Saxons from England to offer glassware, woolen cloth, sword blades and other Western manufactures for silver and spices from Arabia, exquisite Byzantine brocades, ornamented leatherwork from Persia.

The Norwegians, or Norsemen, fearless explorers, subtle lawmakers and callous conquerors, faced west—and pursued their chief adventures on westerly tacks. In the Ninth Century they colonized the largely uninhabited islands of Iceland, the Faeroes, the Hebrides and Orkneys, and occupied half of Ireland, as well as large areas of Scotland and northwestern England. During the 10th Century they set up bases in Greenland and reached the shores of North America around 1000. In Iceland, Norsemen founded a republic run by a parliamentary body called the *Althing*, an extension of the local bodies designed to maintain law and order in their homeland. The Icelandic *Althing*, however, was an island-wide assemblage; it convened once a

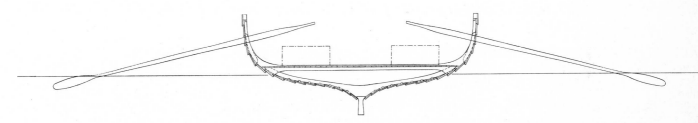

year to pass laws, punish miscreants and to adjust disputes too complex to be settled locally. The *Althing* is the governing body of Iceland today and the West's oldest parliamentary assembly.

While the Norwegians in Iceland governed themselves remarkably well, those peoples who were attacked by them found nothing to recommend the experience. None suffered more or longer than the Celts of Ireland who were under Norse attack or Norse masters for nearly 200 years. Although often defeated and sometimes enslaved or slaughtered in job lots, the Irish were never wholly conquered. By around 1000 A.D. they had driven most of the Vikings from Ireland, although petty wars continued with those who remained. But the Irish were not quick to forgive their depredations. One 12th Century Irish chronicler wrote of the Norwegians with a bitterness as urgent and personal as his ringing rhetoric: "If a hundred heads of hardened iron could grow on one neck, and if each head possessed a hundred sharp indestructible tongues of tempered metal, and if each tongue cried out incessantly with a hundred ineradicable loud voices, they would never be able to enumerate the griefs which the people of Ireland—men and women, laymen and priests, young and old—have suffered at the hands of these warlike, ruthless pagans."

The most advanced and populous of the Scandinavian peoples were the Danes, the major part of whose territory was on a peninsula jutting out from what is now Germany. Less isolated by geography from civilized Europe than the Swedes and Norwegians, the Danes focused their violence on nearby Frankish and English territories—and, as it turned out, with momentous political consequences.

Toward the end of the Eighth Century, Charlemagne's conquests in northern Germany brought him into diplomatic contact with the king of the Danes, who was less than overawed by the mighty Frank. In 810, the Danes went so far as to flout Charlemagne openly, attacking a large part of the Franks' Frisian coast. During the rule of Charlemagne's son, Louis the Pious, the Frankish empire preserved its unity and resisted the Danes' small-scale, probing raids fairly well. But after the death of Louis in 840 the empire steadily disintegrated, opening the floodgates for the Viking deluge.

In 843 the vast and incohesive realm was divided among Louis' three sons under the Treaty of Verdun (*see map, page 106*). One part, an illogically conceived striplike kingdom that stretched from the North Sea to a boundary a little south of Rome, collapsed some 12 years later into an assortment of petty principalities. Another three-way division, arranged by the Partition of Meersen in 870, was more sensible but equally short-lived. In 885 the whole empire was nominally reunited, but it broke up again three years later, this time permanently. Five major divisions resulted; two have endured as countries ever since—France and Germany.

Basically, each new division of the dying Frankish empire meant one thing: a further deterioration of the central power of the Carolingian kings. The monarchs who followed Louis the Pious were all jealous dynasts, blind or unequal to the terrible crises of their times; as they fought each other for land, power and prestige, more and more of their authority and private estates were being usurped by their greedy, irresponsible dukes and counts. With government ailing at every level, continental Europe fell easy prey to the marauding Danes.

In England, the Danish attacks had begun around 835, and in the 840s they increased in size and frequency not only there but on the continent as well. These Viking assaults quickly showed a developing pattern. Instead of a few ships a typical force might now include a dozen vessels with a complement of 600 mariner-warriors. Coming at first only for booty, the Vikings would put ashore near a likely looking town and overwhelm its defenders. Unlike most of the Germanic barbarians of the Fifth and Sixth Centuries whose objective had been to seize land and who had superstitiously avoided churches and churchmen, the Viking raiders made straight for the local church or monastery. Here, they knew, portable wealth would be conveniently concentrated in the form of gold-and-silver reliquaries and other rich sacred objects. Having plundered this treasure, the despoilers usually set the town on fire and made off in their swift ships before the nearest troops could arrive on the scene.

Almost at once, this basic blitzkrieg was broadened to include pillaging on a wider scale. After seizing and sacking a town, the Viking chieftain might post some of his men to guard the beachhead; the rest would steal horses and ravage the surrounding countryside, seeking valuables and also food to sustain further forays. When the raiders chanced to be caught by a well-trained detachment of cavalry, they lost the battle more often than not. But local defense was sketchy at best and steadily deteriorating. Not only were the rulers of Europe preoccupied with fighting each other, the local lords charged with defense were preoccupied with usurping royal properties and with building crude castles to protect themselves from the Vikings and from one another. The European landscape began to assume the medieval look; castle keeps and fortified towns crowned defendable heights and low-lying towns along the coasts and in river valleys girded themselves in protective walls.

Before the 840s had run their course, the Vikings had taken a portentous step. Instead of returning to Scandinavia for the winter and wasting valuable time in transit, they set up semipermanent quarters on islands convenient to their prime plundering grounds, the rich river valleys of England and France. By 855, Viking forces were operating confidently from several such bases at the mouths of the Loire and the Seine and in the Thames estuary. The bases put Viking bands within striking distance of nearly every community, no matter how far inland or upstream. Moreover, the islands would soon be serving as staging areas when the Vikings turned from raiders into invaders and colonizers.

During the next 10 years attacks by the Danes, launched from handy island strongholds as well as from Scandinavia, mounted in a crescendo of violence that did not diminish until the end of the Ninth Century. In those apocalyptic decades Danish fleets, in company with Norwegians, even penetrated the Mediterranean and sacked towns along its shores. One fleet of Danes reached the west coast of Italy in 860, ravished Pisa and—according to Frankish chroniclers—used a cruel ruse to capture a town called Luna, which the Vikings mistook for Rome itself. Claiming that their leader had just died and had been a convert to Christianity, they asked permission to bury him in Luna's church. Once inside the church, the Viking chieftain leaped from his bier, and with his secretly armed men proceeded to pillage the town.

In France, the rising Danish tide is dramatically illustrated by the hapless wanderings of a group of Frankish monks whom the Vikings had driven from their monastery on the island of Noirmoutier at the mouth of the Loire. Carrying precious relics of their patron saint Philibert, the monks fled eastward in search of a safe place to rebuild their monastery. They found a temporary haven in the Loire valley not far from Nantes, but the threat of Viking attacks forced them to move further east in 858—and again in 862, and yet once more about 10 years later. It was not until 875, when they reached the fortified town of Tournus in Burgundy, near the borders of present-day Switzerland, that the refugee monks of St. Philibert found a "place of tranquillity" and settled down for good. One of their members, a monk named Ermentarius, wrote of those terrible times in anguish and despair:

"The number of ships grows larger and larger, the great host of Northmen continually increases; on every hand Christians are the victims of massacres, looting, incendiarism, clear proof of which will remain as long as the world itself endures; they capture every city they pass through, and none can withstand them . . . There is hardly a single place, hardly a monastery which is respected, all the inhabitants take to flight and few and far between are those who dare to say: 'Stay where you are, stay where you are, fight back, do battle for your country, for your children, for your family!' In their paralysis, in the midst of their mutual rivalries, they buy back at the cost of tribute that which

they should have defended, weapons in hand, and allow the Christian kingdom to founder."

Ermentarius' chronicle was accurate on several counts. The number of Viking ships did continue to increase, and dramatically—from large fleets to huge flotillas. Probably the greatest naval assemblage of the age was one that laid siege to Paris around 886, when a reported 40,000 warriors sailed up the Seine in an immense armada of 700 ships. No less significant was Ermentarius' caustic reference to tribute. Some Frankish communities in northwestern Europe had assumed realistically that they would receive no military aid from their king or their local lords in case of Viking attack. Therefore they had begun setting aside a handsome sum to offer the marauders in the vain hope that they would sail away without wreaking slaughter and destruction. This pay-off was gladly accepted by the Viking chieftains, some of whom actually honored the bargain. In 845, for example, 7,000 pounds of silver were paid to expedite the departure of a Viking fleet from Paris. However, one good bribe deserved a return trip for blackmail; before long, paying off the Vikings had become a standard practice on both sides of the English Channel.

In England this payment was known as Danegeld ("Dane-money") and it was in England that it realized its greatest future. Here some of the several petty kingdoms paid the Vikings enormous sums on an annual basis, just like taxes; and, in a frank confession of weakness, the Anglo-Saxons counseled each other, "Buy off the spear aimed at your breast if you do not wish to feel its point." But if paying Danegeld was an ignoble expedient, it proved to be constructive in more ways than one. It not only moderated "the wrath of the Northmen"; it also brought Viking and victim into a *modus vivendi* that would help to unite them.

Around 865, the Danish raids on England had

become a full-scale invasion. Countless Viking bands landed on the east coast, and by 878 their various conquests had been amalgamated into a territory that became known as the Danelaw and which embraced much of central and eastern England *(see map, page 155)*. For more than a century thereafter, warfare was endemic between the Danelaw and the Anglo-Saxon kingdoms to the south and west, and between it and Norwegian-occupied areas in the English northwest. The situation was briefly stabilized by the Anglo-Saxon king, Alfred of Wessex (871-899), the greatest European ruler since Charlemagne and a man much like the Frank in his dedication to the revival of learning. Early in his reign, Alfred came perilously close to succumbing to Viking assaults, and, according to legend, once had to hide out in forests and marshlands until he could recoup his shattered forces. But eventually he managed to unite southern England against the Danes, largely through the force of his personality. As an Anglo-Saxon chronicle put it, "All the English people submitted to Alfred except those who were under the power of the Danes." Confronted by this solid Anglo-Saxon front, Guthrum, king of most of the Danish settlers in England, agreed in 886 to stay behind a fixed boundary. Alfred's peace died with him, but the treaty of 886 remains a milestone in the shaping of Europe. It meant that a Viking kingdom had been recognized as just another belligerent member of the European community.

Alfred the Great was a single bright light in a dark age of European leadership. Not only royal power, but papal prestige as well, neared its nadir in the last decade of the Ninth Century. In Rome, the Holy See fell into the hands of rapacious noblemen, and the popes they installed were mediocrities at best; a full century would pass before the papacy would begin to

regain its moral authority and political influence. In Germany, the Carolingian kings had proved themselves so consistently feeble that in 911 the opportunity to place another one on the throne was turned down brusquely by the dominant dukes. The French Carolingians, no better than their German cousins, somehow managed to hold their throne until 987, when the last king of the once-mighty dynasty was replaced by Hugh Capet, the first of many Capetian kings. But as early as 900, France's reigning Carolingian, Charles the Simple, possessed less power and land than several of his ambitious lords.

In Charles' reign, conditions in northwestern France verged on anarchy. Small armies of Danes, including a liberal sprinkling of Norwegians, roamed at will between the Seine and the Loire Rivers, assaulting the region's oft-ravaged towns and laying waste to its magnificent monasteries. By 911 the king had so little to lose there that he took a fateful gamble.

From the ranks of Scandinavian freebooters, Charles chose one chieftain, Rollo the Viking, and invested him with large tracts of land at the mouth of the Seine. Undoubtedly Charles hoped against hope that Rollo, transfigured with pride in his proprietary status, would henceforth defend his new duchy as ardently as he had ravaged it, thereby barring the length of the Seine to other Viking groups. This gift was both unprecedented and significant, for it initiated a Viking into Western Europe's lordly establishment.

To Charles' contemporaries, his choice of this particular Viking for largess must have confirmed the king's nickname of "the Simple." Rollo was not even a Viking of promise or outstanding valor. Shortly before Charles singled him out, he had put on a dismal show before the walls of Chartres, when for no apparent reason his men had broken off their attack and

GOADED TO FURY *by sticks, massive stallions battle on a carved stone unearthed in Sweden. Horse-fighting was a favorite Viking amusement; the stallion that kicked and bit most fiercely won glory for its owner.*

departed with unbecoming haste. Rollo may have withdrawn because French troops were approaching to relieve the town. Or—as tradition asserts—he may have been routed by the bishop of Chartres, who mounted the town's battlements and waved in the Vikings' faces a garment said to have been worn by the Virgin Mary the night she gave birth to Jesus. Whether Rollo had been battle-shy or superstitious at Chartres, his career had not been one to inspire confidence.

But as it turned out, Rollo and his men proved to be the most important and most adaptable of the Viking bands. Rollo remained surprisingly faithful to Charles, and he fitted perfectly into the hectic milieu of baronial warfare. He and his son quickly expanded the original land grant at the expense of neighboring French lords and guarded it well against Viking rivals. Even before Rollo's grandson Richard took over the domain in 942, the descendants of the Vikings had accepted Christianity, intermarried with the local population and adopted the French language. Already they were being called Normans, a contraction of Northmen, and their territory had become known as Normandy. This hard-boiled duchy was not long in fulfilling its destiny. Richard's great-grandson—who was just five generations removed from Rollo the Viking—was to be the famous Duke William II, the conqueror of England.

While Rollo and his heirs were establishing a kind of rough order in Normandy, the Vikings were obliged to share their European hunting grounds with other rapacious outlanders. Muslim seamen from Spain—bands of the so-called Saracens—established a pirate lair on what is now the French Riviera and for many years terrorized areas of southern Europe. They pillaged far and wide by land and sea and abducted pilgrims on their way to Rome and other holy shrines, holding them for ransom. From the steppes of Asia hordes of nomadic Magyar horsemen burst upon Central Europe and rode in a great circle around the Alps. They cut a swath of destruction through southern Germany, eastern France and northern Italy, tormenting regions that the Vikings had barely touched.

But toward the end of the century the worst was over and Europe was emerging from chaos. Already many local lords had restored a semblance of order in their districts, and it took only a few dramatic events to end the threat of the Magyar and Saracen despoilers. In 955 Otto I, a Saxon who would revive and rule Charlemagne's empire in Germany, dealt the Magyars a decisive defeat near Lechfeld in southwestern Germany, whereupon they retreated eastward and formed the medieval kingdom of Hungary.

The elimination of the Saracen pirates took

somewhat longer. In 972 the pirates overreached themselves by kidnaping and briefly holding Abbot Maiolus of the great Burgundian monastery of Cluny, a personage too august to be trifled with. The monks of Cluny raised the ransom for their abbot, and shortly afterward a strong force of French lords scoured the Riviera and wiped out the Saracen base.

As for the Vikings, their attacks dwindled steadily through the second half of the 10th Century. It is true that as late as the 1020s the Danish king Canute was engaged on a grand scale in conquering and establishing his rule over an empire that included most of England and much of Norway. These military campaigns, however, were no Viking adventure for plunder but simply the aggressive expansion of an ambitious kingdom. Already Scandinavia was an accepted part of the continent, firmly joined to it by the rapid northward spread of Christianity.

The heyday of the Vikings saw its real twilight before the 10th Century was out. By around 1000 the Scandinavian kings and chieftains had exhausted their supply of exportable manpower. In the future Viking warriors might have their fill of adventure in the wars of their kings, in exotic explorations and in long-distance trade. But they were strongly advised, and even enjoined against free-lance raiding and emigration. The original Viking spirit lived on only in literature—in Beowulf and other stirring sagas of the Northmen.

For Europe, the Viking Age had innumerable consequences, both positive and negative. Far to the east the Swedish founders of the trading towns along the Volga and the Dnieper Rivers had soon become installed as official rulers by their Slavic clients. Known to history as the Varangians but calling themselves *Rus*, these expatriate Northmen gave their name to an immense territory and even-

tually they fused their principalities into the first real Russian state, which reached its zenith by the 960s.

To the west, the depredations of Norwegian Vikings in Ireland put a tragic end to three centuries of high Celtic culture; and the Norsemen did little in recompense beyond founding the island's first cities—Dublin, Waterford and Limerick. In France, the Danish Vikings who ravaged the northwest permanently broke up that region's great ecclesiastical estates and crippled its agrarian economy. Yet for France as well as for England and the area now known as the Low Countries, the Northmen worked a constructive economic revolution. The whole western European seaboard—the coasts of the Baltic Sea plus the Atlantic front from Norway to Spain—was united by Viking ships into a single thoroughfare for commerce, a sea route that would soon supersede the Mediterranean in importance to the West.

For these productive results, the Viking Age must be accounted a success, not only for the Scandinavians who benefited by their contact with Europe's more advanced culture, but also for Europe as a whole. In weathering the Viking storm, in taming the Magyars and ousting the Saracen pirates, the continent had concluded its business with the last waves of marauding outlanders. Nevermore would barbarian invaders retard the growth of Europe. The development of its peoples and countries would now go forward at a steadily increasing rate of speed. Indeed, the Viking attacks had forced many fragments of Charlemagne's Europe to adopt, as a makeshift form of government, a new synthesis of old traditions and institutions, feudalism. And upon the political foundations of the feudal system, the unique civilization of medieval Europe was already rising rapidly.

A BEARDED SEAFARER *with menacing teeth, carved in oak, decorates a cart found at Oseberg.*

HOME OF THE NORTHMEN

For centuries the Vikings were known to history mainly through the horrified accounts of their early European victims, who regarded the fierce sea raiders as a scourge sent from God to punish them for their sins. In recent years more dispassionate scholarship, including some remarkable archeological finds, has revealed a fuller picture of the Northmen and the harsh, beautiful land that molded them. How they lived and adapted to their often hostile environment can be glimpsed in various artifacts, from small wooden carvings *(above)* to whole sailing vessels that they buried with their dead. The richest of these finds is the one at Oseberg, Norway, dating from the Ninth Century. Its treasure, which includes a longship, figureheads and sleighs, speaks of a tough, independent people, magnificently skilled in shipbuilding and seafaring, with a lust for exploration and adventure few people in history have ever matched.

Boat-shaped Memorials to Seafaring Men

The Vikings' ships—"steeds of the waves" as poets called them—played such a vital role in their lives that they could not conceive of an afterlife in which ships had no part. Viking chieftains, therefore, were often buried with their ships, in which had been placed provisions for the afterlife, including the bodies of sacrificial animals and even servants. On some occasions the dead man, his ship and all its contents were burned on a huge funeral pyre, ignited by the nearest of kin and fed by the assembled throng of mourners with burning brands. If a boat could not be spared for these ceremonies, stones might be set in the ground in the shape of a ship to insure swift, safe passage to heaven. In the ship burial unearthed at Oseberg, the vessel, thought to have belonged to a Viking queen named Asa, was tied to a rock by a rope, perhaps suggesting that the dead queen was at a safe mooring until she could make the voyage to another world at some future time.

STONES THAT OUTLINE A SHIP *stand on a high moor near the Swedish coast as a memorial to a*

136

forgotten Viking chief. Such monuments, common throughout Scandinavia, are up to 180 feet long; large stones at either end mark the "bow" and "stern."

Long Boats
for Deep Fjords

Since rough, craggy mountains made
up much of their interior landscape and
roads often turned into rivers of mud, the
inhabitants of Scandinavia quite naturally
took to the sea. Villages were usually built
on or near the coast, where deep fjords
offered sheltered harbors; along the
west coast of Norway, a belt of
thousands of islands also helped
to break wild storms and offer
calm sailing. Inevitably the
Vikings' economy depended
on boats, for fishing, for
ferrying supplies of furs
and food and for travel
up and down the coast,
as well as for more
far-reaching voyages
of exploration and
trade. The Oseberg
royal barge, whose
gracefully curving,
elaborately carved
prow is shown at
left, was probably
used primarily
for short coastal
pleasure journeys.

"SERPENT" PROW OF THE OSEBERG SHIP

A FJORD WINDING BETWEEN CLIFFS, *its surface rippled by oar marks as in Viking*

days, cuts through steep rock walls on the Norwegian coast. Such fjords sheltered traders; they also harbored pirates who profited from the traders' cargoes.

Swift Hunting over a Land of Snow and Ice

Long, bitter winters imposed a seasonal rhythm on the life of the Northmen; for almost six months of every year they had to contend with deep snow and freezing cold on land, and foul, icy weather at sea. Farming and maritime activity ceased, and the men turned instead to trapping and hunting, and to the building and repairing of their ships. Much overland travel was done in winter, when lakes, rivers and marshes were frozen over; the ice and snow were turned to advantage with swift conveyances like the horse-drawn sleigh shown below, which was furnished for the eternal convenience of the queen interred at Oseberg. Hunters on crude skis or snowshoes tracked marten, sable, bear, walrus, elk and reindeer for their pelts, ivory and meat. The hides were used for clothing, bedcovers and braided rope, or traded during the summer to inhabitants of southern regions for glassware, silver and silks.

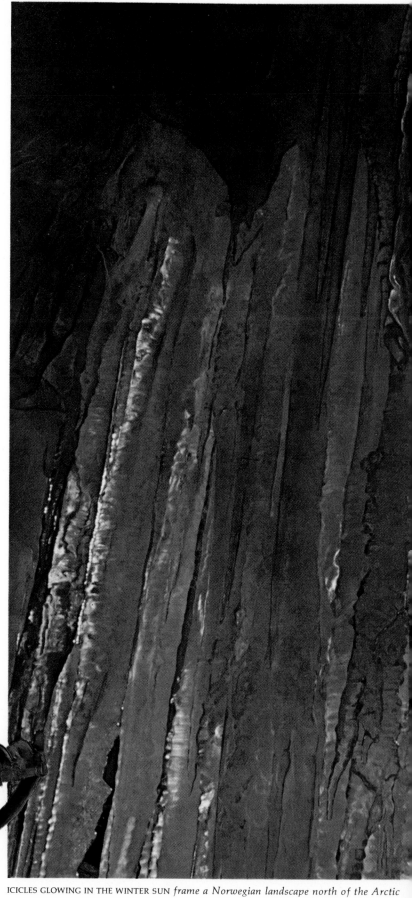

ORNAMENTED VIKING SLEIGH

140

ICICLES GLOWING IN THE WINTER SUN *frame a Norwegian landscape north of the Arctic*

Circle. This region lies under thick snow and ice much of the year, when the earth's north tilts so far from the sun that its light barely appears for days.

VIKING CEREMONIAL CART

Rituals of Flowers
to Welcome the Summer Sun

Because their growing season was so short and its produce so vital, the Vikings, fearful that summer fertility might not come, held elaborate ceremonies each year with the blossoming of spring. They hoped in this way to compensate for their small amount of fertile land, which only Sweden had in abundance.

To herald summer, ornamented carts like the one above were decked with garlands of flowers surrounding a wooden statue of the fertility god, Freyr. Drawn by a horse, the cart went from village to village, as hopeful farmers and their families welcomed it with flowers and sacrifices. If their prayers were answered there would be adequate, if not abundant, supplies of the staples of the Viking diet: wheat and barley, fruit, cabbages and onions, as well as pork and beef. Should crops fail, as sometimes happened, families would be reduced to eating lichen, seaweed and the bark of trees.

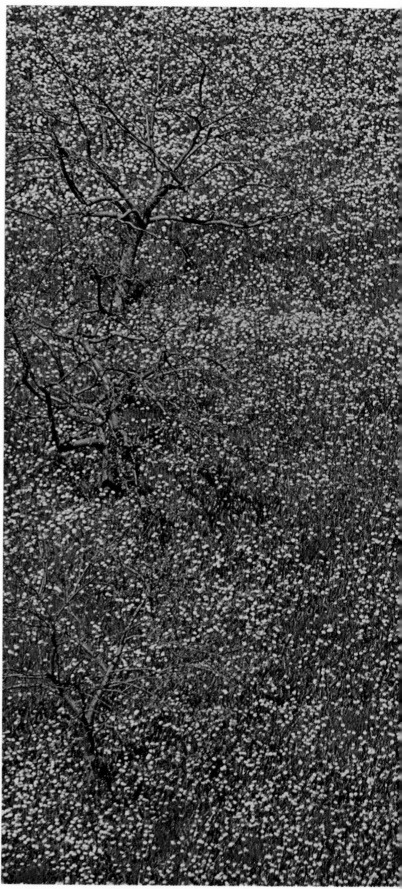

A NORWEGIAN APPLE ORCHARD, *carpeted with yellow spring flowers, offers the welcome*

promise of summer abundance to come. Vikings celebrated the fruitfulness of summer every year at the end of June with dancing and nightlong festivities.

By Dragon Ships
to Stormy, Far-off Shores

After the crops were in the ground and the days grew long and clear enough for sailing, Viking seamen left their families to embark on voyages that might take them to the very edge of the world, where mists obscured vision and ships sometimes mysteriously disappeared. To frighten off foes and evil spirits of the ocean, these mariners sailed under awesome figureheads like the one shown below, which, combined with their vessels' long, serpentine silhouettes, led to the name "dragon ships."

The Northmen were superb shipwrights and ship handlers, and skillful navigators as well. Ship captains had records of landmarks as far west as Greenland; on the open sea they read the sun and stars with crude sighting devices to hold a given course. Few European sailors of the time ventured far from land; the Vikings, however, crossed the ocean to Ireland, Iceland, Greenland—and nearly 4,000 miles to the New World.

DRAGON
FIGUREHEAD

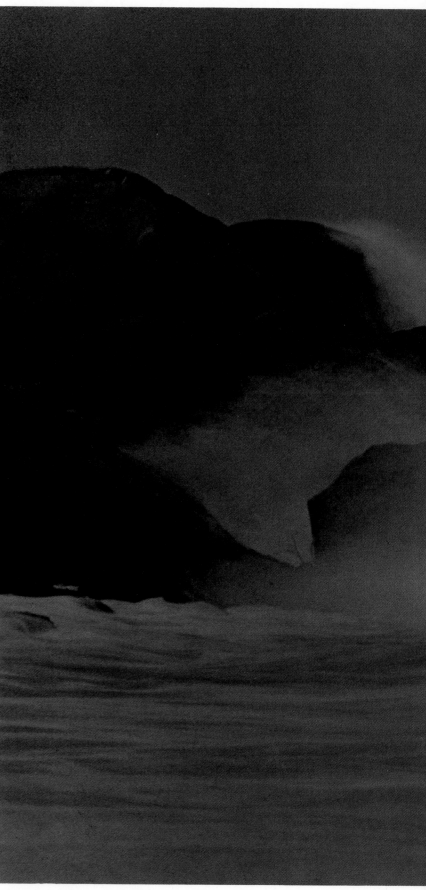

WAVE-BATTERED ROCKS *off North America menaced Viking sailors on their explorations, as*

did Arctic ice and fogs. Nevertheless, growing evidence, including a campsite with iron tools, indicates that they landed more than once in the New World.

7

THE FEUDAL ORDER

WARRIORS OF THE FEUDAL AGE *are seen in the Bayeux Tapestry depicting the Norman invasion of England. The Normans' tightly knit political system, feudalism, insured their conquest of the loosely organized Anglo-Saxons.*

"I will love what thou lovest; I will hate what thou hatest." "As long as I shall live, I am bound to serve you and respect you." "Thy friends will be my friends, thy enemies my enemies."

These startling vows, which bound countless medieval men to their lords, were expressions of that unlikely form of government known as feudalism. Feudalism, whose heyday in Western Europe extended roughly from 900 to 1200, was never planned coherently or adopted universally; it simply developed at random in several regional varieties, each one shaped by and connected to different local institutions. For example, in some areas feudalism was closely linked to the manorial estate, which was farmed for the lord by peasants; in others it was not. Yet for all its anomalies, feudalism had the flexibility and toughness to rescue many regions from imminent anarchy. It provided the stability and the political techniques needed for building strong new central governments. In fact, feudalism was the political solution toward which much of the West had been working unconsciously throughout the Early Middle Ages.

Essentially, feudalism was the offspring of two distinct traditions which had been heading for a marriage from the Fifth Century onward. The older tradition, that of a dependent relationship between two free men, was common to both Roman civilization and Germanic barbarism. During the twilight of the Western Empire, when the floundering Roman state could no longer guarantee the safety of its citizens, many defenseless men appealed for protection to some powerful individual, and received it in return for various personal services, often as armed retainers in his large bodyguard.

The comparable tradition among the Germanic peoples was that of the band of "war companions" —the basic unit of their tribal military organizations. Each band—and a tribe might have several of them—consisted of a war leader and his personal followers. The warriors were dependent on their chosen chieftain for a livelihood in the form of booty, and in return they gave him their fierce loyalty—as long as his leadership served them well.

The Germanic war companion was freer than the Roman armed retainer to switch his allegiance; but the general resemblance between the two, as personal dependents with military obligations, is strikingly borne out by their job names in two languages. The Roman retainer was often called a *buccellarius*, or "biscuit-eater," after the *buccella*, a type of cracker issued to soldiers. Similarly, the Anglo-Saxon war companion was known as a *hlafoetan*, or "loaf-eater." These two "doughboy" traditions came together and naturally reinforced each other after the Germanic conquest.

The second basic component of feudalism was a peculiar Roman tradition of land tenure, which grew ever more crucial as trade declined and land became the only real source of wealth. When the Empire increased its land taxes beyond the financial resources of the small farmers, many of them escaped the crushing burden by deeding their acreage to rich landowners, who then returned the property as a precarium—a "precarious" or temporary holding that was foreclosed at the tenant's death. In practice, the former owner gradually lost his freedom along with the title to his land, becoming a servile or semiservile tenant.

The Germanic tribes had no comparable land tradition of their own. But after the invasions, the kings and war leaders used the Roman formula freely to distribute conquered land among their followers and among the churchmen who became their aides and mentors. To be sure, much land was given free and clear; but by the Sixth Century, most of the peoples of the West were accustomed to the idea that two or more parties could possess different legal rights to the same piece of property.

Since feudalism had its roots in both Germanic and Roman culture, it developed first and most fully in those regions where the two peoples mingled harmoniously. Such was the case in northern France, where the Franks and the Gallo-Romans managed to achieve a rapid, well-balanced and durable integration. It is here, in the heartland of the Frankish kingdom, that feudalism can best be traced

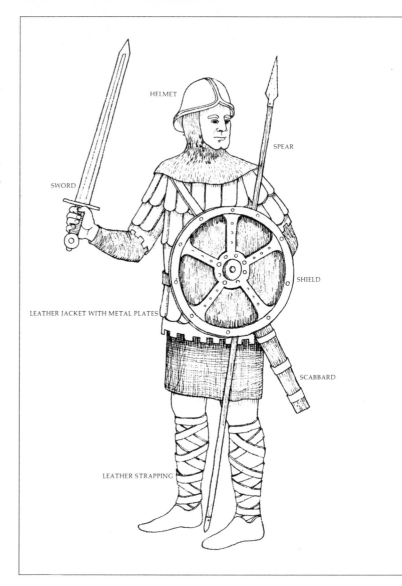

through its early evolution to its vigorous maturity.

During the Sixth Century, conditions in northwestern France created a hothouse climate for feudal growth. Amid continuing economic decline and persistent disorders, more and more free men—small farmers, independent warriors and refugees from abandoned towns—sought protection from the powerful rural military elite, becoming unfree tenants and dependent household warriors on estates of steadily increasing size. As the middle classes melted into the vast substrata of medieval peasants, the last generation of Roman bureaucrats died out, and with them effective government ended.

Now the Merovingian line of Frankish kings faced the overriding political dilemma of the Early

LANCE

HELMET

COIF

MAIL SHIRT

SADDLE

BRIDLE

STIRRUP

SHIELD

SCABBARD

SPUR

IMPROVEMENTS IN ARMOR *in the Early Middle Ages were stimulated by the growing importance of cavalry over infantry. The Eighth Century Frankish foot soldier (left) wore a leather tunic reinforced by heavy, overlapping iron plates and carried a small wooden shield strengthened by metal bands. By contrast, the Norman knight of the 11th Century (right) wore more flexible chain mail; his elongated shield, also of wood with part of its weight supported by a shoulder strap, protected most of his body when he was mounted. His lance, longer than the spear that was a standard arm of the earlier infantrymen, was not only hurled through the air as a javelin, but could also be wielded with deadly effect as a thrusting weapon.*

Middle Ages: how were they to rule far-flung territories without an effective administrative apparatus? The Merovingians had no choice but to award government posts, both secular and ecclesiastical, in the same manner in which they bestowed land: as a conditional lifetime grant to loyal followers. In an important development of feudal tradition, they attempted to acquire service by exacting a solemn oath of loyalty from certain aspirants for office. This pledge made each one a vassal, a term derived from the Celtic word for servant. Counts and bishops became royal vassals, the personal dependents of the king under the same arrangement that bound the household warrior to his landed lord. Thus vassalage was formalized and introduced as polit-

ical policy to the highest levels of government.

To the kings' dismay, however, their beneficiaries treated their gifts—offices and land alike—as permanent, inheritable possessions, and the kings slowly exhausted their own private estates in giving them away as "temporary" but irretrievable gifts. For the Merovingians, the depletion of the royal estates was tantamount to political bankruptcy.

Until the Eighth Century, when the Carolingian family came to power, the traditions of land and of lordship developed without any explicit connection. But the two were recognizably combined by the first of the great Carolingians, Charles Martel, in his bold response to a desperate emergency. In the 720s, repeated incursions by Muslims from Spain forced Martel to mobilize the Frankish kingdom. In order to replenish the supply of royal estates available as inducements for military service, Charles seized many great tracts from the Frankish Church and granted most of the confiscated estates to important lords with many dependent warriors. The actual legal transactions were varied and complex, but Martel's purpose was amply evident: the land was to be used by each lord for raising troops or defraying their expenses; and a precondition for tenure was the lord's pledge of personal loyalty as a vassal. The temporary land grant became an undisguised payment for military service; it later became known as a fief (akin to our word "fee"). With the fusion of vassalage and the fief, feudalism was fully formed, though not yet fully operative.

Charles Martel used his troops as effectively as he had raised them. In 732 he repulsed the Muslims between Tours and Poitiers in a famous battle that marked the debut of the feudal cavalry. The role of Martel's horsemen was severely limited by the technology of the time. The stirrup, which permitted a warrior to fight securely on horseback, would not come into general use in the West until a half-century later; and another century would pass before Europe had a breed of horse large enough to last for long under a warrior weighed down by a heavy coat of iron mail. Nevertheless, Martel's success against the Muslims was a cavalry victory, and one that cast a lengthening shadow.

Almost overnight, the cavalry became the kingpin of medieval warfare. It rose so rapidly in numbers and importance that, by 755, Martel's son King Pepin was obliged to postpone, from March to May, the annual date on which the Frankish armies assembled to launch their sundry campaigns. It took those extra two months of springtime haying to provide enough fodder for all the horses.

The explosive growth of the cavalry created many economic and social pressures, all of which spurred the development of feudalism. The horse now became essential equipment for a warrior of any importance, and horses were expensive. The value of a mount, in terms of status as well as purchasing power, can be accurately estimated by an Eighth Century transaction in which a would-be cavalryman traded his farm and a slave for a horse and a sword. In effect, the small landowner, long a dwindling breed but still respected for his double role as part-time infantryman and part-time farmer, was forced to specialize. If he could not afford a horse, he sank to the level of a mere peasant.

The financial bind was even tighter on the land-rich lords whose households bulged with dependent warriors. Already hard put to feed and outfit his many bully-boys, the lord found it severely taxing to supply them with horses as well. It was actually cheaper, man for man, to invest a warrior with a spare piece of land, which he could exploit as a landholder to provide himself with horse, equipment and maintenance. The granting of a fief to lowly warriors became standard practice in the 10th Century. Thanks to the horse, they started their rise to the honorable and desirable status of knight.

Vassalage increased dramatically in the upper echelons of society during the reign of Charlemagne. The great conqueror doubled the size of the Frankish kingdom, and, in order to staff his government in the new territories, he greatly increased the number of his royal vassals. Counts, dukes, bishops, abbots—all swore lifelong loyalty to their ruler. Yet Charlemagne was well aware of the dangers of extending vassalage as an instrument of central government. He took strong measures to tighten his hold on the royal vassals, and to bind their own vassals to him as well; and he thereby raised the quality of their service. But in improving the performance of his officials, Charlemagne also increased their ability to resist his weaker successors.

Charlemagne's son Louis the Pious, who inherited

the throne in 814, slowly lost the struggle to keep vassalage in harness to the royal government. After Louis, the Frankish empire rapidly crumbled. Its territories were divided and fought for by his sons, and plundered and scourged by Viking marauders. Its central authority died out, leaving nothing behind but the feudal framework that had so long propped it up. Feudalism was finally on its own, and the power it had vested in the local lords was all that stood between society and utter anarchy.

In the second half of the Ninth Century, the Viking attacks ran their violent course. For decades, the defenders were inept and practically helpless. But the local forces slowly triumphed, partly by ejecting some Scandinavian bands, partly by wearing down the invaders through attrition and partly by drawing into the feudal structure such noxious chieftains as Rollo the Viking, who in 911 became a royal vassal, receiving as fief lands that later formed the duchy of Normandy. Feudalism now reached full maturity; this was its so-called classical age.

The hallmark of mature feudalism was a stark, meaningful, three-stage ceremony that wove the many traditions of land and lordship into a single, binding tie. The first ritual was the act of subordination or homage, so called after the French *homme*, or man. The "man"—that is, the junior partner in the lord-vassal relationship—knelt hatless and swordless before his superior or *seigneur* (from the Latin *senior*). He placed his hands in the lord's hands and affirmed his intention to serve the lord for life against "all men who may live or die." The lord indicated his acceptance of the vassal by raising him to his feet and kissing him full on the mouth.

The second ritual, the oath of fealty, intensified the first. The vassal sealed his commitment by swearing complete loyalty and fidelity to his lord; and since he took the oath with his hand on a Bible or on holy relics, any violation would be a sin as well as a crime. Finally, in recognition of the vassal's

service, the lord invested him with a property to provide for his needs in the duties expected of him. The lord often solemnized the grant of a fief with some symbolic gesture—tapping the vassal with a small rod, handing him a pennant or a stick or a clod of earth.

This ceremony represented far more than a rough exchange of land for loyal service. It called into being a complex man-to-man relationship in which both parties had specific legal rights and obligations. The vassal was to respect the lord, promote his interests, attend him in his manor or castle, give him counsel on request, aid him financially in special cases, house him during his periodic visits to the fief and fight at his command for about 40 days a year. In return, the lord was to treat his vassal as an honorable subordinate, assist him in emergencies and seek justice in his behalf. As long as the vassal kept his side of the bargain, the fief was his to use until his death or the lord's. Actually, though the fief and vassal service were uninheritable under feudal law, it soon became customary for the son of a deceased vassal or lord to assume his father's relationship with the survivor.

Custom also conferred on the vassal an extralegal privilege that accounts largely for the indestructibility of feudalism. Every vassal considered it his right to award portions of his fief to warriors of his choice under subsequent contracts. Through such contracts, a warrior could also accumulate several fiefs by pledging vassal service to several other lords. Both practices increased dramatically in feudalism's classical age, and the result was a series of overlapping networks of feudal relationships that might extend from the great *seigneurs* (including the now-diminished kings), outward through several levels of lesser lords. Along these networks, political power centralized or decentralized in an automatic response to changing conditions.

Any sort of crisis—not only armed attack but also

famine or plague—tended to cause a wide diffusion of power and the break-up of fiefs into ever smaller and more easily managed units. In such a cycle, a land-rich lord who could not control his entire holding personally was only too glad to grant fiefs to ambitious warriors, each of whom could better protect the property as a vassal resident on the spot. As a result of repeated subdivision, most fiefs were finally reduced to small estates. For example, one lordlet received as his holding "the third part of the half of two thirds of the tithe [tenth]" of a certain estate—that is, a mere one nineteenth of the original fief.

Despite natural and manmade calamities, however, the capability of the lords themselves was generally the chief factor in determining whether power was diffused widely or concentrated in a few hands. An energetic lord who possessed extraordinary skills as a warrior and organizer could halt almost any centrifugal trend, and even reverse it for his lifetime. The formidable count of Champagne, for example, amassed a great arc of fiefs north and east of Paris by contracting vassal service to the king of France, the German emperor, the duke of Burgundy, two archbishops, four bishops and an abbot. Even then the French count was outdone as a fief-collector by a tireless German warrior, one Siboto of Falkenstein, who served as vassal to no fewer than 20 lords.

Of course the vassal who swore to serve several lords was living dangerously, risking irreconcilable demands upon his loyalty. When obedience to one lord entailed disobedience to another, it could easily provoke a brisk passage of arms. Feudal warfare was an appropriate testing ground, a sure way of proving who was strong in an age when only the strong could be entrusted with the safety of whole communities. If and when common sense prevailed, the vassal pledged to many lords gave first call on his military services to the *seigneur* with the big-

gest, nearest band of knights. Thus strength begat greater strength—until the demise of a mighty lord again disrupted the local status quo.

Clearly a lord's strength depended ultimately on how well he used his fief, personally and to acquire vassal service. Not nearly so clear is the precise nature of the lord's authority over his fief; indeed, this is the elusive essence of feudalism. The average lord had no proprietary rights to his estate. Even the greatest *seigneur* owned very little land outright. He was not a public official authorized to govern the people who lived on his land; no state or political combination existed which could confer such authority. The lord merely received from his *seigneur*—by contract with a private individual, that is—a limited license to use the material resources of the land. In order to take advantage of those resources, he assumed the right to control and exploit the peasants. As for the peasants, they expected no voice in the selection and policies of their lord; they simply needed his services as much as he needed theirs. It took the lord and the peasants to make an estate what it had to be—an autonomous and self-sufficient unit.

The typical estate of the average petty lord started out with the natural defensive advantages that went with small size. A few square miles might be its entire extent: a square mile or so of cultivated land surrounding a village of two or three hundred peasants, surrounded in turn by broad pasturage and then by dense woodlands. The peasants at work in the fields were never far from one of the estate's two strongpoints: the solidly built church in the village and the lord's fortified manor house outside of it. In his primary role as organizer and leader of the local defenses the lord commanded no great force; his manor could support no more than a few household knights. But when a band of invaders was seen breaking through the forest barrier, the lord had time to rally the peasants, who were drilled to follow in support of the professional horsemen. Most battles of the day were little more than brief, crude skirmishes.

The lord's military role had civil extensions. Along with his knights, he kept peace and order and enforced his personal version of the local law, which consisted of customary law plus feudal accretions. Whenever a law was broken, a legal hearing followed promptly, for the lord acted as public prosecutor and chief magistrate as well as policeman for his estate. The verdict of the lord's court was final in all cases not involving major crimes, which his *seigneur* reserved the right to judge.

The object of the lord's civil functions was, of course, to permit the unimpeded pursuit of the estate's indispensable activity—farming. As business boss of the community, the lord planned, and his steward superintended, the labor of the peasants on the manorial lands. Normally, the peasant was required to work a certain number of days each year on the lord's personal acres; this might vary from three days a week to a few weeks a year, depending on the peasant's degree of servitude. He was also called upon to do a variety of other special chores, such as digging drainage ditches and repairing barns. The peasant could spend the rest of his time working on a plot that he considered his own, even though he was no more its owner than the lord himself.

A vital feature of the peasants' labor was its collective character. The peasants necessarily worked together on the lord's fields; and, partly because few of them owned enough oxen to make up a full plowing team, they naturally continued to work together on one another's plots. The actual system of plowing, planting and harvesting varied considerably with local terrain and tradition, but the chief crop was always wheat and other grains that could be ground into flour for making bread.

The lord often used the critical importance of bread to make an additional profit. As part of his economic monopoly, he ran the local mill and oven, charging the peasants a small fee for grinding their grain and baking their bread—and imposing a stiff penalty on any man who dared to have his grinding and baking done elsewhere. The lord also exercised strict control over the timber of the estate, although he did not charge the peasants for the branches that they picked up for their hearths. Otherwise, the lord squeezed some small profit out of everything the peasants did, including marrying and dying. In fact, most lords ran the local church as a profit-making venture: the priest had to pay for his appointment in some fashion, usually by splitting the peasants' tithes with the lord.

Such profit-taking, however, was not necessarily inconsistent with the best interests of the community. While the lord reserved hunting rights in the forest to keep his own table stocked with game, the peasants benefited generally from his woodland restrictions. Because he limited the felling of live trees, the forest remained intact and a good provider. From it the peasants obtained a steady supply of fallen branches for their hearths; and their swine had a steady diet of roots and nuts. Whether the lord was generous or greedy, the natural resources of his estate were woefully meager; and unless their use was carefully regulated for maximum benefit, everyone was bound to suffer.

On a well-run estate, the peasants seldom had cause to traffic with the outside world, even in long periods of relative stability. Occasionally a few men might be sent to another village to sell off some surplus farm animals, or perhaps to bring back a cartload of salt or a special hardwood log from which to fashion replacement gears for the mill. All basic needs, from flour for bread to flax for homespun clothing, were processed in the manorial workshops or in the peasants' cottages.

The basic manorial unit had advantages that

went beyond matters of agrarian self-sufficiency. The government of the small estate was inexpensive. Despite the lord's many rake-offs and minimal public services, it is hard to imagine a form of political organization that could function more cheaply or more efficiently under the circumstances. Just as important, the peasants could identify their best interests with their lord far more easily than with some remote king or disembodied state. Finally, a feudal unit, even one of considerable size, was small enough to be homogenous in language, custom and culture. The great kings had tried and failed to impose unity, from the top down, on vast territories whose peoples lacked any real compatability, much less a natural cohesion. But henceforth the rebuilding of political structures in Europe would proceed logically, from the bottom up. The compact feudal states thus formed would embrace only those areas that had a healthy balance of common characteristics.

In this process, feudalism served many purposes well. As much as we might lament the arrangements that bound men in service to lord and land, these feudal restrictions helped immeasurably to make a place for each man in a stable society. In the desperate feudal centuries, social discipline was a precondition for survival; and, whether the people realized it or not, they subordinated themselves and their old traditions to the needs of the community. For example, the disruptive influence of blood ties, which had led to destructive vendettas since tribal times, was slowly curtailed by the priority of feudal ties, to the benefit of the group and the individual alike.

Feudal relationships were broadening as well as restraining. At every level of society, and across class lines, men necessarily dealt with each other under intensely personal and essentially lawful conditions. In general, feudal ties fostered a sense of loyalty and duty, and even honor and morality.

As early as 843 a Frankish noblewoman named Dhuoda, one of the rare literate ladies of her era, wrote her son William a letter of lofty advice on his new obligations as vassal to King Charles the Bald: "Since God, as I believe, and your father Bernard have chosen you, in the flower of your youth, to serve Charles as your lord, I urge you ever to remember the record of your family, illustrious on both sides, and not to serve your master simply to satisfy him outwardly, but to maintain toward him and his service in all things a devoted and certain fealty both of body and soul."

This spiritual tone was, to be sure, uncommon in feudal relationships before the 11th Century, when it began to infuse the ceremonies of knighthood and the ideals of chivalry. But even the crude minor lords and their cruder vassals shared a manly affection that was just as real as their interdependence. Such sentiments are poignantly attested to in an Anglo-Saxon poem that records the deep grief of a simple household warrior who was deprived of both a generous friend and a protective leader by the death of his lord. In the poem, the forlorn retainer "dreams at times that he embraces and kisses his lord, and lays hand and head upon his knees, as he did in days gone by at the high seat whence bounty flowed; then the friendless man awakes and sees before him now only dark waves. . . . Where are the joys of the great hall? Where, alas, the bright cup?"

Once feudal organization was secure at the local level, it became possible for strong lords to extend their powers over larger areas. Flanders, for example, was little more than a scattering of rural enclaves in Charlemagne's time; but two centuries later, after its thoroughgoing feudalization by a line of iron-handed counts, it emerged as a tightly knit region, advanced and increasingly prosperous.

On the other hand, political development was retarded in those portions of Western Europe where

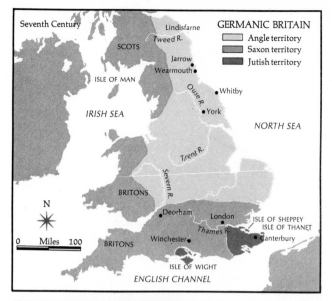

PREY TO INVADERS, *England was first seized by Romans, then by the Germanic Angles, Saxons and Jutes, who divided the land into petty kingdoms. Danish Vikings established a kingdom in England in the Ninth Century; William of Normandy, conqueror of England in the year 1066, united the country under a feudal monarchy.*

feudalization was slow or incomplete. Such was the case in Spain, where rule by the Muslims was a barrier to the spread of feudalism, and in Italy, where a variety of social and economic factors inhibited feudal growth. In Germany, the revival of Charlemagne's empire in 962 by Otto I arrested feudalization; and, although the German empire remained a powerful state until around the end of the 12th Century, it was thereafter steadily outstripped in political progress.

While Germany was looking to the past, a vigorous, forward-looking state was being built on feudal foundations in northwestern France. In the 10th Century, the Norman dukes, descendants of Rollo the Viking, greatly enlarged his original fiefs by employing feudal techniques with dash and expertise. A dynastic crisis in 1035 undid much of their work. But at the same time, it brought to the forefront the master of feudalism, Duke William II—destined to be known as William the Conqueror.

Young William was announced to Norman society in a fashion calculated to forestall trouble. In 1035, as the heirless Duke Robert departed for Jerusalem on a pilgrimage that soon ended in his death, he left behind this gruff command to his vassals: "By my faith, I will not leave ye lordless. I have a young bastard who will grow, please God, and of whose good qualities I have great hope. Take him, I pray you, for lord. That he was not born in wedlock means little to you; he will be none the less able in battle . . . or to render justice. I make him my heir, and I hold him seized, from this present, of the whole duchy of Normandy."

Because William inherited Normandy as a minor, he was powerless at first, and then he had to fight doubly hard to reassert ducal control. In a fine example of feudalism in action, William based his rise on a mutually profitable relationship with clerics of the Norman Church. He favored the reforms of liberal churchmen, gave generously toward the building of new churches and monasteries, and the rebuilding of others that had been destroyed during the Viking invasions. By this policy, William soon acquired the enthusiastic support of his clerical vassals, including Bishop Odo of Bayeux, who later commissioned the famous Bayeux Tapestry. These churchmen helped William to raise, on ecclesiastical estates held as fiefs, a body of knights and soldiers for whom the main chance lay in loyal service to the duke. William used this force to beat down his unruly vassals and to man castles and strongpoints that were built at strategic intervals throughout Normandy. Now no fief was so remote that it could drift off into autonomous limbo, and no vassal was strong enough to break his feudal vows to William without prompt retaliation.

It took William about two decades to complete the job. In that period he not only reconstituted Normandy; he made it the best-organized state that the West had known since the halcyon days of the Roman Empire, some eight centuries before. By 1060 William's feudalized central government was so efficient and secure that surplus warriors—ambitious knights, chronic malcontents and landless second sons—despaired of a future in Normandy and began emigrating to the south. In Sicily, these adventurers used the techniques of Norman feudalism to set up a sophisticated state that incorporated the island's exotic mixture of Muslim and Byzantine institutions.

William was not the man to let his power wither from disuse. The only question was, when and where would he use it? The answer became obvious in 1066, when King Edward the Confessor died heirless in England, leaving that country supremely disorganized, with at least three rivals asserting some sensible claim to the throne. Among the contestants was William of Normandy; Edward had been both his vassal and a relative on his father's side. Duke William prepared to back his claim with force. All the way down the networks of Norman vassalage, the lords began to muster their knights and soldiers for a rewarding campaign.

In the middle of the 11th Century, England was a graphic example of too much fragmentation and too little feudalism. Not that feudalism's potential for political unity had escaped the notice of some kings. For example, Offa of Mercia, Charlemagne's contemporary, had greatly admired Carolingian feudalism and tried to imitate it. But the Anglo-Saxons were practically antisocial in their dogged sense of political and personal independence, and their weak rulers had no way to impose royal authority on great landowners or local officials. In the interests of peace and order, all free men were pointedly advised to submit to some lord; anyone who could not identify himself as the man of lord so-and-so was liable to be slain on the spot as a common outlaw. Such intimidation did little good. The English remained superficially feudalized, resolutely divided and profoundly disorganized—until the Norman invasion in 1066.

If the Early Middle Ages can be said to have ended at one particular time and place, perhaps it was on September 27, 1066, in and around the town of St. Valéry on the French coast of the English Channel. Here, waiting for a favorable tide, was William's potent invasion force of several hundred ships and about 7,000 men. The army included many of the Norman vassals who would soon replace Anglo-Saxons as England's key churchmen and secular officials, important warriors and fiefholders. Within the Conqueror's lifetime, he and his Norman compatriots would feudalize England from top to bottom—and make it an effective state. But this was a political enterprise that properly belongs to another epoch—feudal monarchy on a national scale.

On September 27, the tide turned, and around nightfall Duke William set sail for England.

A TRIPARTITE SOCIETY, *feudalism rested equally on lord and castle, peasant and hut, monk and church.*

THREE FACES OF FEUDALISM

Europe in the 10th and 11th Centuries was a frontier society, fragmented, fearful and rudely fortified against itself. With the collapse of Charlemagne's empire, the last of the orderly centralized governments had disappeared, and a more primitive system had taken over. The basic unit of this system was the village, home to the peasants who supplied each community's food and labor. Frequently the village was defended by a castle, built by the landholding lord and staffed by his retinue of professional warriors. Or the village might be attached to an abbey, whose monks ministered to the spiritual needs of both peasants and lords, and who often had soldiers for their own defense. Together these three groups—described by Alfred the Great of England as "men of prayer, men of war and men of work"—managed to build and maintain a structure that endured through Europe's darkest centuries, until broader, more stable governments could rise again.

Illustrations by Arno Sternglass

The Castle: The Community's Defense

Key to the defense of many feudal communities was a structure called a "motte and bailey" castle, which overlooked the farmlands and nearby village *(upper right)*. The motte, or mound, was built with dirt dug from the ditch that constituted the fort's outermost defense. Atop the motte rose the keep, a building with thick walls and slit windows that served as both watchtower and arsenal, and that contained a well at the bottom, storage and eating rooms above and sleeping quarters on the top level.

In the courtyard, or bailey, stood a collection of sheds used as living quarters for the lord's soldiers, shelters for their horses and storehouses for grain and wine. The outer stone wall, which rose 10 or 12 feet above the bottom of the ditch, had only one gate, reached by a fixed bridge. The keep itself was the last stronghold; equipped with water and emergency supplies, it could sustain the lord and his family, the villagers and the warriors through sieges that might last for months.

The Village: Home of Peasant and Lord

Within sight of the castle guards was the village, around which the peasants toiled, farming the fields and tending the livestock. Most of the fields belonged to the lord, but each peasant was allotted land on which to grow his own grain. He also had a small, fenced-in plot where he maintained his hut, a rude wooden shack with a thatched roof and dirt floor. Here he also had his vegetable garden and, if he were prosperous, an ox, some chickens and a few pigs.

The manor house of the lord *(right)*, somewhat removed from the peasants' dwellings, was larger and more substantially built. It consisted of a ground-level storage area with wood-floored living quarters above, possibly with a stone fireplace and chimney. Surrounding the house were storage barns, live-stock stalls and a stone wall. Usually the focus of village life was the church, facing an open space where women gossiped at the well and where holiday festivities were held. In many communities the church was the only stone building and served as a refuge when the village came under surprise attack.

The Monastery: Keeper of the Spirit

In its tight cluster of stone buildings, the feudal monastery resembled a small city, and indeed it was not only a spiritual retreat but also a many-faceted, self-sustaining town. Outside its walls, peasants tended farms and vineyards; inside, the monks labored over manuscripts and produced furniture, textiles and sacramental objects. Although it was a peaceful community, the monastery and its treasures were not immune to attack; for this reason, it was often fortified.

The center of monastic life was the abbey church, seen here with its tall, massive tower rising behind it. To one side, the main courtyard is surrounded by a cloister, where the monks walked and meditated; a dormitory; a large dining hall; a bakery and a wine cellar. To the right of the dining hall, a dormitory for the novitiates faces another courtyard. Around the perimeter are a number of other buildings, linked by a defensive wall, including a large stable (bottom), an infirmary (top), guest houses, shops, latrines and storage buildings. An abbey of this size could house close to 100 monks, 100 craftsmen and laborers, and as many as 200 wayfarers and visitors, who were guaranteed shelter by the Church.

"It was as though the very world had shaken herself and cast off her old age, and were clothing herself everywhere in a white robe of churches."

This joyful observation, set down around 1050 by the French monk Raoul Glaber, attests to a new spirit that arose in Europe in the 11th Century. This spirit was one of optimism and self-confidence. What is more, it was well grounded on fact. As the Early Middle Ages drew to a close, the peoples of the medieval West had quite suddenly begun to receive big dividends on their ancestors' painful experiments and hard-won gains.

Significant gains were now being registered in every field. Sweeping Church reforms, pressed by such strong popes as Gregory VII, keynoted a general rise in the moral tone of society. In literature, a milestone was marked by the composition in the French language of the great epic poem *The Song of Roland*; the use of the vernacular in this and other works composed soon after reflected and also fostered a growing sense of nationality among many European peoples. Secular education was increasing among the nobility, and even among lesser classes in Italy. Here, as a German visitor noted with admiration and some surprise, it was seldom considered "useless or unseemly to educate a child not destined for an ecclesiastical career."

In the arts, the crowning achievement of the 11th Century was the development of Romanesque architecture. By the year 1100, when the new style reached its solemn maturity, hundreds of Romanesque churches had been built, with a number of brilliant regional variations. In Burgundy and in duchies of southern France, many churches were highly decorated with carvings on portals and capitals. Other regional styles were severely simple. That of Normandy was the most dramatic, featuring somber façades flanked by enormous towers. One of the finest surviving examples of the Norman style is the abbey church of St. Étienne at Caen; dark, powerful and almost brutally plain, St. Étienne seems to capture in stone the very character of the Early Middle Ages.

Underlying all these developments, and doing much to further them, was a phenomenon that made the 11th Century one of the major turning points in world history. This phenomenon was

A GRIM-FACED GUARDIAN *stands before the gates of a fortified town in this ivory bas-relief carved around the year 1000. Already towns were developing, and this urbanization was among the factors—social, political and economic —that vitalized Western Europe toward the close of the Early Middle Ages.*

Europe's economic revival. For six centuries and more, the West had languished under a stagnant economy in which most goods were exchanged by barter. But now it began to experience a galvanic upsurge of money-based commerce. The hard cash pumped into circulation through trade brought about a boom in urban life and, directly or indirectly, it paid not only for the "white robe of churches," but also for docks and market places, roads, bridges and hospitals and, by the beginning of the next century, the first universities.

Europe's economic recovery was the product of innumerable complicated factors. These were so closely interrelated and so sketchily documented by contemporaries that modern scholars find it difficult to assess the relative importance of each, or even to distinguish causes from effects. Among the main factors contributing to recovery were greater output of farm and workshop, the expansion of local and international trade, the birth of new towns and the rebirth of old ones—all activities that began to increase appreciably in the last decades of the 10th Century. During that brief span, just enough stability was restored to Europe to permit the general resumption of such peaceful pursuits after more than a century of depredations by Viking raiders, Magyar horsemen and Muslim pirates. While these pursuits were not resumed in the same sequence everywhere, it seems certain that all owed their new vigor to two basic developments—increased population and improved farm technology.

Both developments had been gaining momentum for some time. An enlarged work force had been building up since the Ninth Century; about that time the excess of births over deaths apparently increased slowly but steadily. Soon afterward, farm production began rising through the cultivation of more land and the use of the three-field system of crop rotation. Men also began rediscovering various simple devices of obscure origin and applying them

to increase the efficacy of labor, both human and animal. One of the first of these devices to be widely adopted in the West was the water wheel; by the end of the 10th Century, numerous mills were using it to harness the energy of rivers and streams for grinding grain and sawing lumber. Among the devices adopted around the same time were the horseshoe and the horsecollar, which allowed horses to exert their full pulling strength, and the heavy wheeled plow, which cut deep furrows and thus was particularly advantageous in the thick damp earth of northern regions.

The effects of rising population and better farming techniques did not become obvious until shortly after the restoration of order in Europe around 960. Then some regions were suddenly producing a precious surplus of agricultural products, freeing their workers from the exigencies of subsistence farming. At the same time other areas had become overpopulated, and their people were forced to till more land to supply basic food needs. In either case, the results were the same: a great increase in constructive new projects.

Countless bands of men went to work in an unprecedented surge of sustained energy. In populous Flanders, large tracts of marshy coastland were reclaimed from the North Sea in an effort to increase arable acreage. In Spain, whole districts depopulated by the wars between Christians and the Muslims were resettled and put to the plow as the so-called Reconquest began driving the infidels southward. Everywhere the age-long work of clearing the forest reached epic proportions, bringing thousands of square miles of land under cultivation.

Organized colonization of tillable lands in Eastern Europe, which had begun in earnest around 800 under Charlemagne, entered a peak period that would last four centuries. Parties of pioneers, most of them from Germany, established new farming communities in what are now Poland and Czechoslovakia. The eastward advance even reached the gateway to the Balkans—Hungary. That country's King Stephen, the first Christian ruler of the kingdom founded by the Magyars, was delighted by the peaceful invasion. In the first half of the 11th Century, he wrote with pride, "Immigrants from different countries bring in different languages, customs, tools and weapons. This diversity is an ornament for the realm, a decoration for the court and an object of fear for our enemies."

Industry as well as agriculture benefited from Europe's increasing surplus of manpower. By the end of the 10th Century, old mines were being worked more intensively and important new ones were discovered and developed, most notably in Germany. Many peasants, some of them craftsmen as well as farmers, began leaving the fields for the workshops in nearby hamlets and for careers as specialists—weavers, tanners, vintners, stonecutters, masons, smiths. This early shift in population, modest though it was, turned the hamlets into small villages and small villages into large ones. As yet, none of these was a town, and many would never become towns because they lacked the commercial activity characteristic of the true urban community. At first the labor of specialized workers supplied only enough wares for local needs, but gradually local commodities were produced in volume sufficient for profitable export. Linen from Italy, fish from Scandinavia, wines from France, cordovan leather from Spain, tin and wool from England, wheat, silver and copper from Germany, woolen textiles from Flanders—these products and more would be well known throughout Europe and beyond by the 12th Century.

The most important of Europe's commodities was the wool cloth from Flanders. Flemish weavers had been famed for their durable fabrics for centuries. As early as the 790s, when Charlemagne wished to send a present to the caliph of Baghdad in return for his exotic gifts of an elephant and a water clock that struck the hours, the great king could choose nothing finer than Flemish wool cloth. Thereafter, Flanders' weaving industry had grown only slowly, retarded by wars and by a shortage of fleece. But by the late 10th Century, the reclaimed marshlands of Flanders had proved unsuitable for farming and were given over to sheep-raising, and the added source of wool gave free rein to the region's weaving industry. More than any other single product, Flemish cloth stimulated the growth in Europe of international trade, which medieval men came to call "grand commerce," to distinguish it from local trade.

Long-distance trade had been minor in scale and chiefly maritime in character since before the fall of Rome. The international merchants of early medieval times brought from the East luxuries (mostly spices) for the West's few wealthy lords and churchmen, and they returned to the East with the West's few lucrative commodities (mostly furs and slaves). They made their journeys along the main traditional waterways of trade: the southern or Mediterranean route, between Constantinople and north Italy; and the northern route, which ran from Constantinople through the Russian river system to the Baltic Sea, the North Sea and the English Channel. A trickle of trade had continued to flow along both routes despite Muslim control of the Mediterranean Sea and Viking violence in northwestern Europe. But as European commodities increased in variety and volume, the East-West trade grew from a trickle to a steady stream. By the end of the 10th Century, the success of European products, especially Flemish wool cloth, had established a sound basis for an innovation of vital significance: an overland trade route cutting through the heart of the continent to connect Flanders and northern Italy.

In the 11th Century, Europe's economic revival

gained momentum rapidly; long-distance trade supplied its impetus, and before long the Flanders-Italy route became the main axis for its new gains. More and more great merchants added the trip across France to their annual itineraries. Soon it became their custom to stop off en route to transact their business in a half-dozen fairs held in rotation in the Champagne region of eastern France, whose central location made it a natural rendezvous for traders from as far as Scotland and North Africa. At these colorful fairs, foreign wares passed directly to buyers and also to small traders with regional routes. The small traders in turn distributed them to peddlers with local routes; and the same process in reverse started domestic wares on their outward journey. Inland Europe was slowly being knit together by an ever-expanding network of trade.

The early medieval merchants left behind scant records of their genius for commerce; but one trader, the Englishman Godric of Finchale, was rescued from anonymity by his pious philanthropy, which won him canonization and an idealized biography written in the 12th Century. According to his admiring biographer, St. Godric scaled the ladder of business success in a career of only 16 years. He started out as a youthful peddler who was "wont to wander with small wares around the villages and farmsteads of his own neighborhood." Graduating to regional trade, Godric "did so profit by his increase of age and wisdom as to travel . . . through towns and boroughs, fortresses and cities, to fairs and to all the various booths of the marketplaces." Then, as a long-distance merchant, Godric traded in Scotland, Denmark, Flanders and Italy; "he made great profit in all his bargains, and gathered much wealth in the sweat of his brow . . ." Before he donated his entire fortune to the poor and became a hermit, Godric "purchased the half of a merchant ship with certain of his partners in the

trade; and again by his prudence he bought the fourth part of another ship."

Important merchants such as Godric needed depots along their routes, workmen to unload and store their wares, craftsmen to maintain their ships and wagons. These simple essentials for an expanding trade were largely responsible for the most spectacular aspect of Europe's economic revival—the birth of new towns and the rebirth of old ones.

By the 10th Century, urban life in Europe had been in eclipse for some 400 years. The towns of the Roman West, overpopulated and underproductive by the Fifth Century, had failed to survive the food stoppages caused by the ensuing barbarian wars; townspeople everywhere were forced to abandon their homes and spread out through the countryside, there to grow their own food or perish. Between 410 and 560, the population of the West's greatest city, Rome, was reduced from nearly a million to a few thousand wretches living off papal alms. The trend toward ruralization was hard to reverse even after agricultural production again became sufficient to support urban life.

At the end of the 10th Century, genuine urban life probably existed in less than a dozen towns on the entire European continent, and none with a population as large as 10,000. A hundred years later there were several dozen towns, a few of them with 20,000 residents or more. And this was merely the beginning of an urban boom that in the Late Middle Ages would see European cities growing at roughly the same rate as American cities did in the 18th and 19th Centuries.

The chief towns to burgeon with commerce in the 11th Century included Rouen and Paris in France, Hamburg and Cologne in Germany, and Venice, Genoa, Pisa and Amalfi in Italy. The actual pattern of urban growth, however, varied greatly from region to region, and most importantly between the northern territories and those of the Mediterranean south. The southern regions possessed numerous very old townsites that still retained remnants of their citizenry; commercial activity animated these existing centers first, and few new towns were needed for some time. For example, Nîmes in southern France, whose shrunken population lived huddled together within the walls of its Roman amphitheater, expanded again in the 11th Century and assumed a place of modest importance in the Rhone valley trade. Venice, founded in the Fifth Century by refugees fleeing barbarian invaders, grew into a commercial center that would have no equal for more than a century. As a nominal subject of the Byzantine empire, Venice had been granted a preferred position in Constantinople's Italian trade, and it was by exploiting this grant that the Adriatic port grew populous, prosperous and mighty.

In sharp contrast to the south with its many ancient townsites, the northern regions' old towns were few and far between. Here new towns proliferated, built up virtually from scratch, without benefit of a vaguely remembered urban tradition. These were the towns of Europe's future. In their painful growth and their vigorous life, we can discern perhaps the first recognizable signs of urban civilization as we know it today.

The merchants who founded the northern towns were not building for the ages. These great wholesalers, whose business kept them traveling most of the year, merely wanted bases for transshipping their goods and for waiting out the winter months. But the selection of a base site was no haphazard affair, the principal requirements being that it provide convenient access to a major trade route and military protection. In practice, groups of merchants usually set up their depots in a good harbor or on a navigable river and outside the walls of a burg, or fortified administrative center, of an important lord or a high churchman. Such merchants'

A HERITAGE OF WORDS

Scholars in the Early Middle Ages, represented by this 11th Century drawing of St. Matthew, devoted themselves to the art of making books. Many English words stem from the period, including "book" and "clerk."

BOOK—from the Anglo-Saxon "boc," or "beech tree." Early English priests are believed to have written their runes on thin beech bark.

CLERK—originally a slurred pronunciation of "cleric." In medieval times, clergymen were usually the only ones sufficiently well educated to perform clerical or secretarial work.

GOSPEL—derived from the old English "god spell," signifying "good tidings," and applied later to "God's story"—the life of Jesus.

GOSSIP—from "godsip," an old term for godparents, who would often gossip about the family to which they were "related in God."

PATTER—a slurred version of "pater noster," the opening words from the Lord's Prayer. Many parishioners did not understand Latin.

settlements, which were soon enclosed in walls of their own, were called *faubourgs* (suburbs) or new burgs. Their residents came to be called burghers—or burgesses or bourgeois—to distinguish them from the inhabitants of the old burgs, who were known as *castellani* (castle-dwellers).

Many merchants' enclaves soon produced a radical change in local life for as much as 30 miles around. Their markets attracted lords and peasants, who sold or traded foodstuffs and other farm products for wares that they had ceased to make for themselves. The new burgs offered many new opportunities for work and profit, capturing as residents craftsmen from neighboring villages, free peasants discouraged by the farmer's lot, unfree serfs fleeing their economic bondage, small traders and local peddlers, drifters and shady characters from all over Europe. Swelled by this motley influx, the new burgs became thriving communities—dense mazes of wooden buildings set cheek to jowl along dark, filthy, crooked alleys. In Flanders, many a merchants' town soon engulfed the burg that had protected it and burst through its successive rings of outer walls at 50- or 100-year intervals.

Along with the blessings of commerce, the burgeoning towns of both northern and southern Europe presented social and political problems of staggering difficulty. These problems were especially numerous and acute in the north where few precedents existed for urban and commercial life. Also, feudalism in its strongest form held sway there and with its rural and military orientation was fundamentally incompatible with towns and trade. At first, none of the leaders of northern societies had workable answers to such basic questions as the legal status of the burghers and the political jurisdiction under which a town fell. The problems were resolved in the usual medieval fashion, by improvisation and a long clash of wills rather than by policy or plan. In the process, every segment of society paid a high price in suffering for a general improvement in the human condition.

Who, exactly, were the burghers? Most of them were men of humble background, but it was hard to determine whether any specific individual was a freeman or a serf, each of whom was judged differently. Certainly the townsmen as a group fitted into none of the three accepted categories of early medieval society—those who fought, those who prayed and those who tilled the soil. Who was to govern—or at least to control—the brawling burghers and their crime-ridden towns? Presumably the responsibility fell to the lord or bishop whose stronghold had served as the town's nucleus. But under what law and by what means was he to exert his power? Feudal law might be applied to settled farmers and to warriors bound to their lords, but it was virtually useless for merchants seeking payment from delinquent debtors who might abscond on the morrow. Moreover, military force had severe limitations as a long-term means of imposing order on a few thousand resentful, footloose burghers. At first the townsmen did not ask to govern themselves, only to be permitted to ply their trade without interference; but they could not be governed passably without their cooperation.

For the conservative leaders of northern societies, the towns represented a clear threat to their authority, their beliefs and their privileges, and they responded accordingly. Most feudal lords seized every opportunity to harry and humiliate the burghers. Many high churchmen viewed the merchants with suspicion and distaste, partly because trade necessarily involved money and credit extended at interest—the Church at that time banned the charging of any interest whatsoever. One English monk, chorusing the general clerical opinion, condemned the merchants and their growing trade as "a bloated swelling of the people, a terror of the kingdom, a wet blanket on the Church."

Gradually, however, the leaders of society found ways and means of reconciling themselves to the towns. The clerics had only to acknowledge the Church's commitment to serve all mankind; just as earlier priests had become aides and mentors to the crude barbarian kings, so many a churchman taught and led in town councils as the ambitious burghers struggled to police their own affairs. The kings, alert to all possibilities for improving their diminished position, were often quick to appreciate the political value of the towns with their rising concentrations of wealth and population. The kings of England and France, who contrived in the 12th Century to gain the allegiance of their towns, were thereby able to extend their authority despite the usual resistance of their feudal lords.

As for those noblemen, their hard hostility toward the towns was soon softened by their hearty appetite for gain. The taxes and tariffs they levied on the merchants, and the huge sums they realized by selling local trade monopolies and limited privileges in the form of town charters, gave many lords a prodigal income, permitting them to equip elegant retinues and to replace their fortified wooden manor houses with drafty stone castles. And yet the instinctive hostility of the feudal lords toward the towns had been correct in the first place—at least as far as their own interests were concerned.

The revival of urban and commercial life triggered a social revolution that was to prove fatal to feudalism. To be sure, feudal institutions and practices would persist for centuries in many regions. But nothing could prevent the business-minded burghers from winning the geographic mobility essential to their trade, or from establishing a new social mobility. Both of these triumphs inexorably undermined the restrictions vital to feudal regimes. The townsmen became a new class of society, a "middle" class that by the mid-11th Century began closing the age-old social gap between the rural military elite and the toiling peasantry. In less than a hundred years, rich men who had been born peasants would begin buying, for mere money, great estates that bankrupt lords had held by virtue of warrior service. More and more unfree serfs would disrupt the balance of manorial life by running away to the towns. At first they sought only a higher standard of living, not liberty for its own sake; notions of personal and political freedom were still too rudimentary for that. But the seeds of such notions were beginning to sprout, and the towns nurtured them. In many regions the tradition grew that any man, however servile his origins, became a freeman simply by living in town for a year and a day.

Besides freedom, other vague ideas and feelings were astir in Europe. These sentiments, like urban and commercial life, were just beginning to mature as the Early Middle Ages came to an end, but already their future had been assured, largely as a result of the patient teachings of the Church. Among the sentiments was a belief in the dignity of labor and the sanctity of the individual. Also, a genuine respect for all law was growing, fostered in part by the desire of merchants to conduct their trade unhindered by highwaymen or pirates. The chances for a better life had now manifestly improved, and because life therefore had greater value, more men longed for a stable environment in which to explore the new possibilities. The desire for peace, order and better government was fast becoming a common ideal. Indeed only one ardent hope of medieval men had no future whatsoever: that of unitary rule inherited from imperial Rome and now clad in Christian clothing. Although the Europeans' sense of Christian unity was keener in the 11th Century than ever before, never had Europe been divided into more political fragments —and such belligerent fragments at that.

For medieval men, the momentous gains of the

11th Century were by no means clear. But in the long view of history, the main thrust of that hectic era is unmistakable, whether it be called the acculturization of the barbarians or the founding of European civilization. The numerous peoples of the West had by then developed a capacity for purposeful action, without which no culture can make real progress or even preserve the gains of the past. The Romans had lost this faculty in the Fourth Century, and without it they had been unable to prevent their Western Empire from crumbling away. But in the 10th and 11th Centuries, the descendants of the Roman citizens and the Germanic barbarians had finally taught themselves how to use their enormous energies effectively—to make war better, regrettably, but also to build better, and above all to function well in communities that were growing ever more varied and complex in social grouping and political organization. For some six centuries, the Europeans had struggled along in dread of some new barbarian invasion; but now several of their societies possessed the resources and the self-assurance, based on actual accomplishment, to launch invasions of their own.

In these adventures, the Europeans were aided to no small extent by a general decline within the two cultural blocs with which they shared the medieval world—Byzantium and Islam. In intellectual and artistic development, both these great societies were still well ahead of Europe in the 11th Century. But both were sorely afflicted by sundry diseases. The Byzantine empire, which had made no real political or social progress for centuries, had entered a period of territorial shrinkage and would disappear entirely with the fall of Constantinople to the Ottoman Turks in 1453. Monolithic Islam was a thing of the past; its fragments, disrupted by religious disputes and civil wars, lacked the strength and will for concerted resistance.

The weakness of Byzantium and Islam was capitalized on by the Europeans in the second half of the 11th Century. The prospering cities of Italy, whose self-made rulers entertained territorial ambitions worthy of anointed kings, carried the battle to the Muslims, attacking their ports and decimating their fleets at sea. Up-and-coming Genoa and Pisa seized Muslim-held Sardinia and Corsica, while Venice appropriated sections of the Balkan coast. Meanwhile, bands of northern warriors from the duchy of Normandy projected themselves recklessly onto the southern scene. Among their conquests were parts of southern Italy claimed by Byzantium and the Muslim stronghold of Sicily; the Normans even seized a long strip of the North African coast. The assorted triumphs over Islam made the entire Mediterranean safe for Christian trade and travel. It also set the stage for that grandiose drama, the First Crusade.

In 1095, when Pope Urban II exhorted all men of Christian Europe to free the shrines of the Holy Land from the infidel, his call to arms meant different things to the warriors who took up the Cross. To all, by papal dispensation, it was a guarantee of the soul's salvation. To many who put mundane ambitions ahead of spiritual redemption, it offered an irresistible opportunity to win fame, or collect booty, or carve out new estates, or rule whole countries—or just to escape the humdrum in glorious adventuring.

But whatever motives prompted warriors to embark for the Holy Land, the First Crusade proved exactly how far the peoples of the West had come in six centuries. They were now capable of uniting in a common cause, of cooperating on a continental scale despite their internal hostilities. This merely confirmed the recent trend. In terms of political, social and economic development, leadership in the medieval world was passing to Europe, and the Europeans would show no signs of relinquishing it for centuries to come.

GOD THE JUDGE *sits enthroned above a lamb symbolizing Christ (center) in a medieval illustration.*

THE APOCALYPTIC VISION OF AN AGE

Beset by catastrophe, the men of the Early Middle Ages sought to find a sense of order in their perilous world. The ideas they developed were imaginative and, in harmony with the times, stark, ominous and simplistic. The everyday world and the spiritual world, heaven and hell, angels and demons—all were equally real, equally important. All actions were subject to divine scrutiny, certain to be rewarded or punished in the Last Judgment as foretold by the Book of Revelation. Learned interpretations of the Book of Revelation, combined with vivid illuminations such as these taken from an 11th Century Spanish edition, reveal brilliantly the haunted landscape of the medieval mind.

Photographs by Augusto Maneses

Repent; or else I will come unto thee quickly . . . and all the churches
shall know that I am He which searcheth the reins and hearts: and
I will give unto every one of you according to your works.

ADVISING AN ANGEL, *St. John, author of Revelation, passes on a divine warning for parishioners of an early church (above, right).*

For the medieval faithful, life on earth was a harrowing struggle between good and evil, a battle whose outcome would decide their fate in the more important life hereafter. From itinerant preachers and their own priests, the people heard dire warnings against sin, many of which were based on Revelation, and they took literally the descriptions of the supernatural agents that would punish sins. Disbelief was a terrible risk, for at the Last Judgment, when God consigned each man to heaven or hell according to his own actions, the torments of the damned would continue forever.

Acceptance of such stern teachings was natural in early medieval times, when life was harsh indeed. The disasters brought by the Four Horsemen of the Apocalypse *(right)* were familiar visitations, afflicting righteous and iniquitous alike "with sword, and with hunger, and with death, and with the beasts of the earth." The faithful could hope to be saved by repentance. But the warring forces in Revelation, and the very nature of medieval life, made man's future seem very grim.

THE FOUR HORSEMEN OF THE APOCALYPSE *ride forth to scourge mankind. Behind the fourth rider, Death, flies a creature named Hell.*

DEMONIAC LOCUSTS, *described in Revelation as horselike, are summoned up by an angel to torment men who have been faithless.*

The great day of His wrath is come. . . . Woe, woe, woe, to the inhabiters of the earth

According to Revelation, many signs of divine retribution would warn mankind of the impending doom. Among the catastrophes were famines, earthquakes, plagues and eclipses, some of them heralded by the trumpet blasts of angels. Fortified by this holy text, priests and their parishioners were quick to attribute to the direct intervention of divine power the full range of natural phenomena—a logical conclusion in a day when no other rational explanation was able to account for illness and health, storm and sunshine. Even the scrupulous scholar Bede, foremost historian of early medieval England, revealed himself as a man of his times when he automatically accepted as a divine act an epidemic so virulent that "the living were scarcely sufficient to bury the dead."

No less an authority than Pope Gregory the Great warned that "these signs of the end of the world are sent before . . . that we may be solicitous for our souls, suspicious of the hour of death, and may be found prepared with good works to meet our Judge."

CELESTIAL TRUMPETERS, *portending the Last Judgment, announce manifestations of God's wrath. A flaming mountain (above) was cast into the sea, and below, "the third part of the sun was smitten, and the third part of the moon . . . and the day shone not."*

And there appeared a great wonder in heaven

Biblical scholars, seeking moral and historical lessons in Revelation, interpreted its mysterious symbols in terms of good and evil. In one

view of the passages illustrated above, the woman "clothed with the sun" *(top, left)* represents the Church, bulwark of the faithful against evil. The threatening dragon, routed from heaven by angels, is Satan, who is shown at lower right caged and chained in Hell.

*Her sins have reached unto heaven. . . . Therefore shall her
plagues come in one day, death and mourning, and famine; and she shall
be utterly burned with fire; for strong is the Lord God who judgeth.*

A DOOMED WOMAN, *representing "Babylon the great, the mother of harlots," rides a monster while holding aloft a golden cup.*

The Book of Revelation not only foretold the terrible punishment awaiting a sinful world—an all-consuming holocaust—but also suggested when it might come. The approach of the Last Judgment was to be announced by God's destruction of man's greatest works, represented by illustrations of Babylon drawn in two forms, as an idealized city of sin and as a wealthy harlot. The book mentioned an actual date: "when the thousand years are expired." This passage aroused some fear that doomsday would fall on the millennial anniversary of the Nativity, and as 1000 A.D. approached, a few fiery preachers toured churches practically guaranteeing the end of the world. Nevertheless, the year appears to have passed uneventfully, and along with it the worst of man's pious fears.

UBI BABILON. ID EST

ISTE MUNDUS ARDET

SYMBOL OF WORLDLINESS, *the city of Babylon dies in flame—punishment for having "glorified herself, and lived deliciously."*

And I saw a new heaven and a new earth: for the first
heaven and the first earth were passed away. . . . And I John
saw the holy city, new Jerusalem, coming down from God.

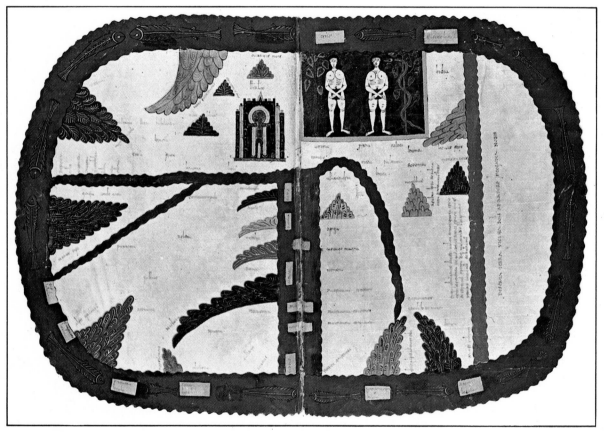

A FANCIFUL MAP *of the world doomed by God shows Adam and Eve atop continents surrounded by waterways, fish and islands.*

St. John's visions in Revelation end after the Last Judgment when the prophet is granted the thrilling sight of God's Heavenly City. An eternal life in this glorious realm was a prize medieval men could win only by lives of righteousness. But their pious hopes for heaven and fears of hell had already earned them rewards on earth before the Early Middle Ages drew to a close. By the 11th Century, men had been raised by Church tutelage to a growing appreciation of the Christian ethic. Their governments were now soundly based on the doctrine that man-made laws were an earthly manifestation of divine justice, and obedience to law was therefore considered man's religious duty. On these Christian foundations, Europe was to make dazzling progress in the centuries ahead.

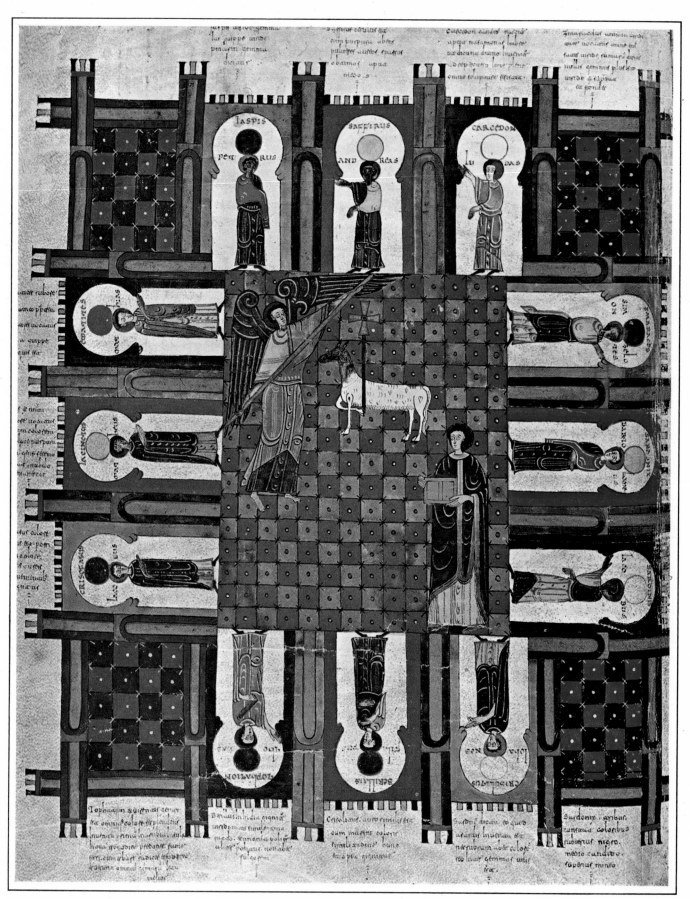

THE CITY OF GOD, *with 12 pearly gates, descends from heaven to receive the blessed, for whom "God shall wipe away all tears from their eyes."*

CHRONOLOGY—*A listing of significant events during the Early Middle Ages*

716 St. Boniface (Winfrith of Wessex) leaves England to begin his great missionary career

c. 725 Charles Martel mobilizes the Franks to stem the advance of the Muslims from Spain; he seizes Church lands to pay his soldiers

732 The Muslims are defeated near Poitiers, and Charles Martel becomes the Christian hero of the West; Boniface is consecrated archbishop

741 Charles Martel dies and his son Pepin succeeds him as mayor of the palace; Pepin invites St. Boniface to reform the Frankish Church

751 Pepin, with the consent of Pope Zacharias, deposes the last Merovingian king and becomes first of the Carolingian monarchs

c. 755 Under the Donation of Pepin, the king of the Franks cedes to the papacy lands wrested from the Lombards

768 Pepin dies, and the Frankish crown passes to Charles the Great or Charlemagne

773 Charlemagne invades Lombard Italy

774 The Lombards are defeated by Charlemagne who makes himself their king

778 Charlemagne campaigns in northern Spain; during his return Count Roland is killed in the Pass of Roncesvalles

c. 780 The Spanish monk Beatus writes his commentary on The Book of Revelation

782 Alcuin of York joins Charlemagne's court and heads the palace school at Aachen

784 Charlemagne subdues the Frisians of the North Sea coast

789 First Vikings attack England, according to Anglo-Saxon chroniclers

796 Charlemagne deals a decisive blow to the Avars, invaders from Asia

797 Irene becomes Byzantine empress after usurping the throne from her son, Constantine VI, among doubts that a woman could legally rule the empire

c. 799 Charlemagne completes his submission of the Saxons in northeastern Germany

c. 800 Vikings from Norway invade Ireland; the Carolingian minuscule style of handwriting begins to be adopted throughout the Frankish Empire; Charlemagne builds his famous chapel at Aachen

800 Pope Leo III crowns Charlemagne emperor of the Romans

802 Empress Irene is overthrown and a male ruler mounts the Byzantine throne

810 Danish Vikings attack Frisia but are driven off

812 Michael I, the Byzantine emperor, recognizes Charlemagne as his imperial "brother"

814 Charlemagne dies and his son Louis the Pious becomes emperor

c. 820 Eginhard writes his biography of Charlemagne

c. 825 Swedish Vikings establish bases on the Volga and Dnieper in Russia, leading to Scandinavian trade with Constantinople and the Near East

c. 835 The Danes begin their attacks on England

840 Louis the Pious dies, dividing the Carolingian empire among his three sons

PERIOD OF SECOND BARBARIAN INVASIONS

c. 840 Viking attacks on England and the continent start to increase in size and frequency; Norwegian Vikings found Dublin in Ireland

843 The Treaty of Verdun redivides the Carolingian empire of Louis the Pious among his three sons, Lothar, Charles the Bald and Louis the German

855 Viking raids are being launched from island bases in France and England

860 Danes and Norwegians penetrate the western Mediterranean, reaching Pisa and Luna in Italy

c. 865 The Danes begin a full-scale invasion in England

870 Part of the kingdom of Lothar is divided between Charles the Bald and Louis the German

871 Alfred the Great becomes king of Wessex

878 Alfred suffers a major defeat in a surprise Danish attack

c. 880 Norwegian colonists settle Iceland

884 The Carolingian empire is reunited for the last time under Charles the Fat

886 The Anglo-Saxons, led by Alfred, make peace with the Danish leader Guthrum; Alfred recognizes the boundary of the Danelaw; a reported 40,000 Vikings besiege Paris

888 Charles the Fat dies and the Carolingian empire is permanently partitioned

c. 890 Magyar hordes from Asia start invading Central Europe

c. 900 The feudal system begins to take shape in many parts of Europe

910 The great Burgundian monastery of Cluny is founded

911 Carolingian line comes to an end in Germany; Charles the Simple grants land in northwestern France to Rollo the Viking

c. 915 Saracens set up a pirate lair on the French Riviera

930 Norwegians in Iceland establish the Althing, a parliamentary assembly

955 The Magyars are defeated by the German king Otto in the battle of Lechfeld

962 Charlemagne's German empire is revived under Otto I

972 Saracen pirates kidnap the Abbot of Cluny, after which their Riviera base is destroyed by French nobles

c. 985 Norwegians build bases in Greenland

987 The last Carolingian on the French throne is succeeded by Hugh Capet, first of the Capetian dynasty

PERIOD OF COMMERCIAL AND URBAN REVIVAL

c. 1000 Norwegian Vikings reach the North American coast; Venice, already a great commercial center, begins to expand along the Dalmatian coast of Yugoslavia

1001 Stephen I is crowned first Christian king of Hungary

1016 The Danish conqueror Canute becomes king of England

c. 1020 The city-states of Genoa and Pisa seize Corsica from the Muslims

1035 William, a descendant of Rollo the Viking, becomes duke of Normandy

c. 1062 The Romanesque church of St. Etienne is begun at Caen

c. 1065 The merchant Godric of Finchale is born

1066 Edward, king of England, dies and William of Normandy launches the conquest of England

1073 Gregory VII becomes pope

c. 1075 Wool-manufacturing towns of Flanders become major factors in the revival of European trade

c. 1090 "The Song of Roland" is composed in medieval French, making it the first great epic written in a Romance language

1091 Normans complete conquest of Muslim-held Sicily

1095 Pope Urban II exhorts Christian warriors to liberate the Holy Land from the Muslim infidels; the First Crusade begins

BIBLIOGRAPHY

The following volumes were selected during the preparation of this volume for their interest and authority, and for their usefulness to readers seeking additional information on spe- cific points. An asterisk (*) marks works available in both hard cover and paperback editions; a dagger (†) indicates availability only in paperback.

GENERAL HISTORY

Arbman, Holger, *The Vikings*. Ed. and transl. by Alan Binns. Frederick A. Praeger, 1961.
Bark, William Carroll, *Origins of the Medieval World*.† Doubleday Anchor Books, 1960.
Bloch, Marc, *Feudal Society*.* Transl. by L. A. Manyon. 2 vols, University of Chicago Press, 1961.
Brøndsted, Johannes, *The Vikings*.† Transl. by Kalle Skov. Penguin Books, 1965.
Bullough, Donald A., *The Age of Charlemagne*. G. P. Putnam's Sons, 1965.
Burns, D. Delisle, *The First Europe*. W. W. Norton, 1948.
Bury, J. B.:
    History of the Later Roman Empire.† Vol. I. Dover Publications, 1958.
    The Invasion of Europe by the Barbarians.* Russell & Russell, 1963.
The Cambridge Medieval History. Vols. I-III. Cambridge University Press.
Cantor, Norman F., *Medieval History*.* Macmillan, 1963.
Coulton, C. G., *Medieval Panorama*.† Meridian Books, 1955.
Curtis, Edmund, *A History of Ireland*.* 6th rev. ed. Barnes & Noble, 1950.
Deanesly, Margaret, *A History of Early Medieval Europe from 476-911*. Barnes & Noble, 1963.
Dill, Samuel, *Roman Society in Gaul in the Merovingian Age*. Barnes & Noble, 1966.
Douglas, David C., *William the Conqueror*.* University of Chicago Press, 1964.
Fichtenau, Heinrich, *The Carolingian Empire*.* Transl. by Peter Munz. Barnes & Noble, 1963.
Ganshof, F. L., *Feudalism*.* Transl. by Philip Grierson. Harper & Row, 1964.
Hay, Denys:
    Europe: The Emergence of an Idea.* Harper Torchbooks, 1966.
    The Medieval Centuries.* Harper Torchbooks, 1966.
Joyce, Patrick W., *A Social History of Ancient Ireland*. 2 vols. Dublin, M. H. Gill & Son, 1920.
Lopez, Robert S., *The Birth of Europe*. M. Evans & Co.-J. B. Lippincott, 1967.
Lot, Ferdinand, *The End of the Ancient World and the Beginnings of the Middle Ages*.* Transl. by Philip and Mariette Leon. Harper Torchbooks, 1965.
McEvedy, Colin, *The Penguin Atlas of Medieval History*. Penguin Books, 1967.
Owen, Francis, *The Germanic People*. Bookman Associates, 1960.
Pirenne, Henri:
    Economic and Social History of Medieval Europe.† Harcourt Harvest Books, 1956.
    Mohammed and Charlemagne.* Barnes & Noble, 1955.
Rice, David Talbot, ed., *The Dawn of European Civilization: The Dark Ages*. McGraw-Hill, 1965.
Simpson, Jacqueline, *Everyday Life in the Viking Age*. G. P. Putnam's Sons, 1967.
Stenton, Frank, *Anglo-Saxon England*. 2nd ed. Oxford University Press, 1963.
Stephenson, Carl, and Bruce Lyon, *Medieval History*. Harper & Row, 1962.
Strayer, Joseph R., *Western Europe in the Middle Ages*. Appleton-Century-Crofts, 1955.
Strayer, Joseph R., and Dana C. Munro, *The Middle Ages, 395-1500*. 4th ed. Appleton-Century-Crofts, 1965.
Thompson, E. A., *The Early Germans*. Oxford University Press, 1965.
Wallace-Hadrill, John M., *The Barbarian West, 400-1000*.† Harper Torchbooks, 1962.

INSTITUTIONS AND TRADITIONS

Bainton, Roland H., *Christendom*, Vol. I, *From the Birth of Christ to the Reformation*.† Harper Torchbooks, 1966.
Dawson, Christopher H., *Religion and the Rise of Western Culture*. Sheed & Ward, 1950.
Gilson, Etienne, *History of Christian Philosophy in the Middle Ages*. Random House, 1955.
Hoyt, Robert, ed., *Life and Thought in the Middle Ages*. University of Minnesota Press, 1967.
Laistner, M.L.W., *Thought and Letters in Western Europe, A.D. 500-900*.* Cornell University Press, 1957.
Latourette, Kenneth Scott, *A History of the Expansion of Christianity*, Vol. II, *The Thousand Years of Uncertainty, A.D. 500-A.D. 1500*. Harper & Row, 1938.
Lovejoy, Arthur O., *The Great Chain of Being*.* Harper Torchbooks, 1960.
Kern, Fritz, *Kingship and Law in the Middle Ages*. Transl. by S. B. Chrimes. Oxford, Basil Blackwell, 1956.

McNally, Robert E., *The Bible in the Early Middle Ages*.† Newman Press, 1959.
Morrall, John B., *Political Thought in Medieval Times*.† Harper Torchbooks, 1962.
Pirenne, Henri, *Medieval Cities*.† Doubleday Anchor Book, 1956.
Walker, Williston, *History of the Christian Church*. Rev. ed. by C. C. Richardson and others. Scribner, 1959.

ART AND ARCHITECTURE

Bieler, Ludwig, *Ireland, Harbinger of the Middle Ages*. Oxford University Press, 1966.
Conant, Kenneth J., *Carolingian and Early Romanesque Architecture*. Penguin Books, 1959.
Henry, Françoise:
    Irish Art in the Early Christian Period (to 800 A.D.). Cornell University Press, 1965.
    Irish Art During the Viking Invasions (800-1020 A.D.). Cornell University Press, 1967.
Hinks, Roger, *Carolingian Art*.* University of Michigan Press, 1962.
Kidson, Peter, *The Medieval World*. McGraw-Hill, 1967.
Paor, Maire and Liam de, *Early Christian Ireland*. Frederick A. Praeger, 1964.
Ross, Anne, *Pagan Celtic Britain*. Columbia University Press, 1967.
Volbach, Wolfgang Fritz, *Early Christian Art*. Harry N. Abrams, 1962.
Wilson, David M., and Ole Klindt-Jensen, *Viking Art*. Cornell University Press, 1966.

TECHNOLOGY AND ECONOMICS

Brøgger, A. W., and Haakon Shetelig, *The Viking Ships, Their Ancestry and Evolution*. Transl. by Katherine John. Knud K. Morgensen Publishing, 1953.
The Cambridge Economic History of Europe. 2nd ed. Vols. I-III. Cambridge University Press.
Latouche, Robert, *The Birth of Western Economy*.* Transl. by E. M. Wilkinson, Barnes & Noble, 1961.
Thompson, James Westfall, *Economic and Social History of the Middle Ages*. 2 vols. Frederick Ungar, 1966.
White, Lynn, Jr., *Medieval Technology and Social Change*.* Oxford University Press, 1962.

CONTEMPORARY SOURCES

Adam of Bremen, *The History of the Archbishops of Hamburg-Bremen*. Transl. by Francis J. Tschan. Columbia University Press, 1959.
Augustine, Saint, *City of God*.* 2 vols. Transl. by John Healey. Dutton, Everyman's Library, 1945.
Bede, *Ecclesiastical History of the English Nation*. Transl. by John Stevens. Dutton, Everyman's Library, 1960.
Beowulf. Ed. and transl. by Charles W. Kennedy. Oxford University Press, 1940.
Easton, Stewart C., and Helene Wieruszowski, *The Era of Charlemagne*.† Anvil Original, 1961.
Einhard, *Life of Charlemagne*.† University of Michigan Press, 1960.
Eirik the Red, and Other Icelandic Sagas. Ed. by Gwyn Jones. Oxford University Press, 1961.
Fredegar, *Chronicle of Fredegar*. Transl. by J. M. Wallace-Hadrill. Humanities, 1960.
Gregory, Bishop of Tours, *History of the Franks*. Transl. by Ernest Brehaut. Octagon Books, 1965.
Jordanes, Bishop of Ravenna, *The Gothic History of Jordanes*. 2nd ed. by Charles C. Mierow. Barnes & Noble, 1960.
Salvian, *The Writings of Salvian, the Presbyter*. Transl. by Jeremiah F. O'Sullivan. Cima Publishing Co., 1947.
The Song of Roland.† Transl. by Frederick Bliss Luquiens. Collier Books, 1967.
Snorri Sturluson, *Heimskringla: The Norse King Sagas*. E. P. Dutton, 1948.
Tacitus:
    The Annals of Imperial Rome.* Transl. by Michael Grant. Penguin Books, 1956.
    On Britain and Germany.† Transl. by H. Mattingly. Penguin Books, 1962.
Whitelock, Dorothy, and others, eds., *The Anglo-Saxon Chronicle*. Rutgers University Press, 1961.

ACKNOWLEDGMENT OF QUOTATIONS

Page 14: St. Cyprian, from *The Birth of Europe* by Robert S. Lopez, M. Evans and Company-J. B. Lippincott Company, 1967, p. 25. Pages 115, 116, 118, 121, 122: from *The Song of Roland*, transl. by Frederick Bliss Luquiens, reprinted with permission of The Macmillan Company, 1952. Page 126: from *Beowulf*, transl. by Charles W. Kennedy, Ox- ford University Press, 1940, pp. 9-10. Page 129: from *The Vikings* by Johannes Brøndsted, Penguin Books, 1965, p. 58. Page 131: Ermentarius, from *The Birth of Western Economy* by Robert Latouche, Barnes & Noble, 1961, p. 217. Page 154: from *Feudal Society* by Marc Bloch, University of Chicago Press, 1961, p. 183.

ART INFORMATION AND PICTURE CREDITS

The sources for the illustrations in this book are set forth below. Descriptive notes on the works of art are included. Credits for pictures positioned from left to right are separated by semicolons, from top to bottom by dashes. Photographers' names that follow a descriptive note appear in parentheses. Abbreviations include "c." for century and "ca." for circa.

COVER—Replicas of the *Morse Chesspieces* from Isle of Lewis, Outer Hebrides, Scotland, carved whalebone ivory, 12th c., courtesy British Museum, London (Fred Eng). 8-9—Map by Nicholas Fasciano (Robert S. Crandall).

CHAPTER 1: 10—Detail of *Helmet Plaque* of Agilulf, King of the Lombards, gilt copper, late 6th c., Museo Nazionale del Bargello, Florence (Ann Münchow). 12—Map by Rafael D. Palacios. 17—Lettering by Donald and Ann Crews. 19—Caricature of a Roman by a Gaul, etched on marble slab, 4th c., Musée de Montmaurin, France (Yan). 21-31—Details from *Column of Marcus Aurelius*, Piazza Colonna, Rome, 180-183 A.D. (David Lees).

CHAPTER 2: 32—So-called *Throne of Dagobert*, bronze folding chair, early 9th c., from Abbey Church of St. Denis, courtesy Bibliothèque Nationale, Paris. 34—Map by Rafael D. Palacios. 36—*Diptych of Stilicho*, ivory, ca. 400 A.D., Cathedral Treasury, Monza, Italy (Alinari). 43—Disc with horseman, Germanic, bronze, 6th c., Badisches Landesmuseum, Karlsruhe, Germany (Pierre Belzeaux from Rapho Guillumette). 44-45—Detail from *Gundestrup Cauldron*, Scandinavian, silver, 1st c. B.C. to 3rd c. A.D., National Museum, Copenhagen (Larry Burrows); Viking head, carved elkhorn, 11th c., Statens Historiska Museum, Stockholm (Pierre Belzeaux from Rapho Guillumette); human figure from Irish bowl found in Viking grave, Norway, bronze and enamel, 9th c., Bergen Museum, Bergen, Norway (Pierre Belzeaux from Rapho Guillumette). 46-47—Portion of a belt buckle, Merovingian, gold with polychrome enriched with jewels, 7th c., Musée des Antiquités Nationales, Saint Germain-en-Laye, France (Pierre Belzeaux from Rapho Guillumette)—two bird appliqués from a shield, silver gilt with garnets, ca. 600 A.D., courtesy Trustees of the British Museum, London. 48-49—Two copies from the *Torslunda Plaques*, Scandinavian, bronze matrices, 7th c., The Museum of National Antiquities, Stockholm (Heinz Zinram). 50-51—Detail from *Frank's Casket*, Anglo-Saxon, whalebone ivory, 7th c., courtesy Trustees of the British Museum, London. 52—*Vendel Helmet*, Viking, iron and bronze, 7th c., Statens Historiska Museum, Stockholm (Pierre Belzeaux from Rapho Guillumette). 53—Two swords, Viking, iron and bronze, 9th and 10th c., courtesy University Museum of National Antiquities, Oslo. 54—*Cesana Bird Brooch*, Ostrogothic, gold and precious stones, cloisonné technique with almandines, early 6th c., Germanisches National Museum, Nuremberg, Germany (Pierre Belzeaux from Rapho Guillumette). 55—Votive crown of King Recceswinth, Visigothic, gold filigree with pearls and sapphires, 7th c., National Archeological Museum, Madrid (Augusto Meneses).

CHAPTER 3: 56—Symbol of St. Mark from Echternach Gospel, probably Irish, illuminated manuscript, ca. 690, courtesy Bibliothèque Nationale, Paris. 60—*Werden Reliquary Casket*, oak covered with carved bone plaques, 7th or 8th c., Abbey Church of St. Liudger, Essen-Werden (Ann Münchow). 67-79—Photographs by Evelyn Hofer.

CHAPTER 4: 80—Lawgivers, illuminated manuscript, early 9th c., courtesy Benedictine Abbey of St. Paul, Carinthia, Austria. 85—Miniature from Aelfric's paraphrase of the *Pentateuch* and *Joshua*, 11th c., courtesy Trustees of the British Museum. 87—Door knocker, bronze, ca. 1140, courtesy Dean and Chapter of Durham, England (Heinz Zinram). 88-89—*St. Andrew's Reliquary*, gold set with precious jewels, 10th c., Trier Cathedral Treasury (Bildarchiv Foto Marburg). 91-99—Details from the Canterbury Psalter, illuminated manuscript, 12th c., Trinity College, Cambridge, England (Alan Clifton).

CHAPTER 5: 100—*Charlemagne*, stucco mold of 9th c. statue, Church of St. Johann de Munstair, Grisons, Switzerland (Ann Münchow). 106-107—Maps by Rafael D. Palacios. 108—Four evangelists from *Book of Kells*, illuminated manuscript, Irish, late 8th or early 9th c., Trinity College Library, Dublin (Heinz Zinram for TIME); script page from *Book of Kells*, illuminated manuscript, Irish, late 8th or early 9th c., Trinity College Library, Dublin (Heinz Zinram for TIME)—portrait of St. Mark from *Ada Gospel*, illuminated manuscript, Carolingian, ca. 800, Stadtsbibliothek, Trier (Wolfgang Braunfels); Eridanus from *Aratus manuscript*, illuminated manuscript Harley 647, Carolingian, mid-9th c., courtesy Trustees of the British Museum, London—initial from *Sacramentary of Archbishop Drogo of Metz*, illuminated manuscript, Carolingian, ca. 842, Bibliothèque Nationale, Paris; evangelist portrait from *Gospel Book of Archbishop Ebbo of Rheims*, illuminated manuscript, Carolingian, before 823, Bibliothèque de la Ville, Épernay, courtesy Bibliothèque Nationale, Paris—story of Adam and Eve from *Great Bible of San Paolo Fuori le Mura*, illuminated manuscript, Carolingian, 9th c. (Scala); Annunciation to the Shepherds from *Book of Pericopes of King Henry II*, illuminated manuscript, Ottonian, 11th c., Bayerische Staatsbibliothek, Munich. 113-123—Details from Window of Charlemagne, stained glass, early 13th c., Cathedral of Chartres, France (Pierre Belzeaux from Rapho Guillumette).

CHAPTER 6: 124—Details from buckle of sword belt, Scandinavian, gilt silver inlaid with niello, gold and garnets, 7th c., University Museum of National Antiquities, Oslo, Norway (Pierre Belzeaux from Rapho Guillumette). 127—Map by Rafael D. Palacios. 128-129—Drawings by Enid Kotschnig in consultation with William Baker, Naval Architect and Curator, Hart Nautical Museum, Massachusetts Institute of Technology, Cambridge, Massachusetts. 133—Detail of picture stone showing stallion-baiting, Scandinavian, sandstone, 400-550 A.D., Statens Historiska Museum, Stockholm (Heinz Zinram for Time). 135—Carved head on wooden cart from *Oseberg Find*, Viking, 9th c., Viking Ship Museum, Oslo (Dmitri Kessel). 136-137—Photograph by Ernst Haas. 138-139—Prow of Oseberg Ship, Viking, carved oak, 9th c., Viking Ship Museum, Oslo, courtesy Universitetets Oldsaksamling, Oslo; photograph by Pete Turner. 140-141—Sleigh from Oseberg Find, Viking, carved oak, 9th c., Viking Ship Museum, Oslo, courtesy Universitetets Oldsaksamling, Oslo; photograph by Pete Turner. 142-143—Cart from *Oseberg Find*, Viking carved oak 9th c., Viking Ship Museum Oslo (Dmitri Kessel); photograph by Pete Turner. 144-145—Dragon figurehead from *Oseberg Find*, Viking, 9th c., Viking Ship Museum, Oslo (Dmitri Kessel); photograph by Leonard McCombe.

CHAPTER 7: 146—Detail from Bayeux tapestry, 11th c., Bayeux Museum, Bayeux, France (Erich Lessing from Magnum). 148-149—Drawings by Nicholas Fasciano. 155—Maps by Rafael D. Palacios. 157-163—Drawings by Arno Sternglass.

CHAPTER 8: 164—Detail from holy-water font, carved ivory, ca. 1000, Aachen Cathedral Treasury, Aachen, Germany (Ann Münchow). 169—St. Matthew, illuminated manuscript, 11th c., Bibliothèque Royale de Belgique, Brussels (Bildarchiv Foto Marburg). 173-183—*Beatus Apocalypse Manuscript*, from *San Isidore de Leone*, Ms. B. 31, early 11th c., Biblioteca Nacional, Madrid (Augusto Meneses).

ACKNOWLEDGMENTS

For help given in the preparation of this book, the editors are particularly indebted to Karl F. Morrison, Associate Professor, Department of History, University of Chicago. The editors are also indebted to Jeremiah F. O'Sullivan; Nancy Wolsk; Harry Bober, Avalon Foundation Professor in the Humanities, Institute of Fine Arts, New York University; W.T.H. Jackson, Professor, Department of Germanic Languages, Columbia University; Helmut Nickel, Curator, Arms and Armor, The Metropolitan Museum of Art; Rev. Ladislaf Orsy, S. J., Professor, Theology Department, Fordham University; William A. Baker, naval architect, Curator, Hart Nautical Museum, Massachusetts Institute of Technology; Colonel John R. Elting, U.S. Army; John Plummer, Research Fellow of Art, William M. Voelkle, Assistant Curator, Medieval and Renaissance Manuscripts, Louise Houllier, Supervisor, Photographic Records, and Richard E. Priest, Supervisor, Reading Room, The Pierpont Morgan Library; Robert Branner, Professor, Department of Art History, Columbia University; Rev. Paul V. Callahan, S. J., Regis High School, New York City; Roland H. Bainton, Professor Emeritus, Yale Divinity School; Ramón Menendez Pidal, President of the Spanish Royal Academy of Letters and member of the Royal Academy of History, Madrid; Matilde Lopez Serrano, Director, Library of the Royal Palace of Oriente, Madrid; Felipa Niño, Executive Secretary, National Archeological Museum, Madrid; Trinity College Library, Cambridge University, England; The British Museum, London; René Joffroy, Conservateur en Chef, Musée des Antiquités Nationales, Saint Germain-en-Laye; Giselle Sarrazin, Chargé de Mission, Musée des Antiquités Nationales, Saint Germain-en-Laye; Bianca Maria Felletti Mai, Director, Museo dell' Alto Medioevo, Rome; Luciano Berti, Director, Museo del Bargello, Florence; Wolfgang Braunfeld, Professor, Kunsthistorisches Institut, University of Munich; Fridolin Dressler, Bayerische Staatsbibliothek, Manuscripts Room, Munich; Hirmer Verlag, Munich; Ann Münchow, Aachen; Rev. Bernhard Knapp, O.S.B., Benedictine Abbey of St. Paul, Carinthia, Austria; Lars Lagerqvist, Curator of Education, and Maj Odelberg, Assistant Curator of Education, Museum of National Antiquities, Stockholm; Sven-Erik Norin, District Custodian of Antiquities, Linköping, Sweden; The Museum of National Antiquities, Lund University, Lund, Sweden.

INDEX

* This symbol in front of a page number indicates an illustration of the subject mentioned.

✕

PRODUCTION STAFF FOR TIME INCORPORATED

John L. Hallenbeck (Vice President and Director of Production),
Robert E. Foy, Caroline Ferri and Don Sheldon
Text photocomposed under the direction of Albert J. Dunn and Arthur J. Dunn